Quilts
from Lavender Hill Farm

Darlene Zimmerman

©2008 by Darlene Zimmerman

Published by

kp **krause publications**

An Imprint of F+W Publications

700 East State Street • Iola, WI 54990-0001
715-445-2214 • 888-457-2873
www.krausebooks.com

Our toll-free number to place an order or obtain
a free catalog is (800) 258-0929.

The following registered trademark terms and companies appear in this publication:

A&E Threads®, Bernina of America®, Companion Angle™, Country Quilting, Country Roads
Machine Quilting, Countryside Quilting, Daffodil Hill Vineyard, Easy Angle™, Easy Scallop™,
Equilateral 60-Degree Triangle™, EZ Quilting by Wrights®, Fairfield Processing Corp.®,
Flip-n-Set™, Hobbs Bonded Fibers®, Robert Kaufman Fabrics, Inc.®, Roxanne's glue Baste-It,
Stone Ridge Quilting, 45-Degree Diamond™

Library of Congress Control Number: 2006935762

ISBN-13: 978-0-89689-436-5
ISBN-10: 0-89689-436-3

Designed by Rachael Knier

Printed in China

12 11 10 09 08   6 5 4 3 2

Dedication

This book is dedicated to Judy Phipps, whose gentle and giving nature make any place feel like home. Thanks for sharing your beautiful home with all of us.

Acknowledgments

No man (or woman) is an island, and this book would never have been produced without the help of my wonderful friends. Thank you!

* Judy Phipps, for sharing her lovely Daffodil Hill Vineyard with us.

* Judy Hillman, for bringing me to Daffodil Hill Vineyard, inspiring me to write this book, and for all her help styling the quilts in the photo shoot.

* Sarah Hillman, for her fabulous expertise with a camera, who made each photograph a work of art.

* Rachel Shelburne, for her precise and beautiful illustrations.

* Candy Wiza, my acquisitions editor, for smoothing the way and guiding the whole process.

* Rachael Knier for the lovely book design.

* Jay Staten for all her help and expertise.

* Margy Manderfeld for letting me use her "Perfect Fit" binding technique.

* Barb Simons at Stone Ridge Quilting for quilting FROSTY MORNING.

* Lois Sather at Country Quilting for quilting SWEET DELIGHTS.

* Cindy Larson at Country Roads Machine Quilting for quilting WILD ROSES.

Thanks to the following companies for all their help:

* Robert Kaufman Fabrics, Inc., EZ Quilting by Wrights, Bernina of America, A&E Threads, Fairfield Processing Corp., and Hobbs Bonded Fibers.

Table of Contents

Introduction

WELCOME TO LAVENDER HILL FARM

Welcome! I would like to invite you to visit Lavender Hill Farm which is nestled in the picturesque Willamette Valley of Western Oregon. This is one of the most peaceful and beautiful places you can imagine. I was visiting my friend Judy Hillman in Salem, Oregon, and we had planned to spend a lovely summer day visiting rose gardens in the city, after a short visit to a lavender farm. A farm that grows lavender—what a delightful picture this conjures up! That brief visit lasted until dusk. The scents, the sounds, and the views were so enchanting we could not pull ourselves away. The farm inspired me to write this book and create the quilts that were photographed in this beautiful setting.

The farm is a very special place to visit. As you wander up the gravel driveway, the vista of the green rolling hills in the distance and the old-fashioned climbing roses that entwine around the split rail fence bordering the drive invite you to linger. At each bend in the road there are charming vignettes of flower beds, bird houses and garden seats. Arriving at the restored farmhouse, you are greeted by the sight of a small greenhouse filled and surrounded by flowers. Beyond that is glimpsed a whimsical henhouse, complete with happy hens! To one side of the greenhouse is an old-fashioned barn/studio that is redolent of the lavender products stored and sold there. The barn loft, a working studio, is a delightful sunlit room with inspirational vistas from all the windows. There is a sunny hillside next to the farmhouse that is blanketed with

lavender plants. What a fabulous sight and a heavenly scent! I fell in love with the farm, and if I lived there I would never leave, not even to buy groceries.

The owner, Judy Phipps, is a professional sculptress and painter (www.judyphippsartist.com). She welcomed us graciously with warm blueberry muffins and tea, followed by a tour of the farm, which in real life is called Daffodil Hill Vineyard. (Because I saw the lavender fields in bloom, to me the farm will always be called *Lavender Hill Farm*.)

Daffodil Hill Vineyard was once a fruit farm with an orchard of cherry trees, but most of the land is now given over to grapes for local wines. A hillside of wonderfully scented lavender is planted near the farmhouse, and harvested in the summer months to make various lavender-based creams and cosmetics, as well as sold fresh and dried by the bunch.

A new addition to the farm is a quaint guest house with an old-fashioned front porch that overlooks the gardens and the lavender hillside, while behind the guest house you can see acres of grapes. The house, barn, guest house, porches and gardens are all delightful, making this a heavenly place to spend a day…or a lifetime. You can visit online at www.lavendergoods.com.

I invite you to walk with me through the pages of this book to experience the peaceful beauty of this lovely Lavender Hill Farm.

General Instructions

CHOOSING FABRIC

Publishing a book is a long process. Even though the very latest fabrics are used in this book's quilts, identical fabrics may no longer be available. Don't despair! Choose similar fabrics if you like the original quilt, or be daring and choose a different colorway for an interesting variation.

Whatever fabrics you choose, try to buy the best quality. Quality fabrics will be easier to sew and you will have a better finished product. The colors will last longer, and the fabric will hold up well to wear and tear.

PREPARING THE FABRIC

You may choose to prewash your fabric—or not. It is a personal decision. The fabric will lose some body and you may have some shrinking and raveling. You can restore the body with a little spray starch or fabric sizing, but don't leave such products in the finished quilt long-term, they may attract dirt and bugs.

You can test a fabric for color bleeding by spritzing a small area with water then ironing it right sides together with a white fabric. If there is color transference, it would be safer to prewash.

Ironing the folds out of the fabric is a necessary step for accurate cutting.

CUTTING

Accuracy in cutting is important for the pieces to fit together properly in your quilt. Some tips for accurate cutting:

• Work in good light, daylight if possible.

• Iron the fabrics before cutting.

• Cut only two layers of fabric at a time. Any time saved in cutting more layers will be lost when trying to fit together the inaccurate pieces.

• Keep your tools from slipping. Use the film or sandpaper that adheres to the back side of the tools.

• Use a sharp rotary cutter and a good mat. Mats and cutting blades do wear out over time, so replace them as needed.

USING THE TOOLS

Suggested tools are listed for most of the patterns. They will make your cutting easier and more accurate, but if you choose not to use the tools, alternate cutting directions are provided.

The tools are not interchangeable! Use the correct tool to cut the shapes. A tool tutorial is given on pages 118–123 so you can learn to use them properly and understand where to use the tools. They are meant as all-purpose tools for use with any quilt project.

CUTTING TABLES IN THE PATTERNS

Most of the patterns have cutting tables. The first column of the tables will tell you which fabric to cut. The second column will tell you how many and what size strips to cut from those fabrics, and then, in the third column, what shapes to cut from each strip.

SEWING

Quarter-inch seams are so important! If at all possible, find a quarter-inch foot for your machine, made specifically for quilt piecing. They are well worth the small investment.

If you have problems with the "mad feed dogs" chewing up your fabric, try these tricks to tame them:

- Insert a new needle, a sharps or quilting needle, an 80/12 would be a good size.

- Clean and oil your sewing machine, particularly under the throat plate.

- Chain-sew whenever possible.

- Begin and end with a scrap of fabric.

Tip

Try this quick check to see if you are sewing an exact ¼" seam allowance: Cut three 1½" x 3½" strips. Sew them together on the long edges. Press. The square should now measure 3½." If not, adjust your seam allowance. (Also check that you have pressed correctly.)

UNSEWING

It's a fact of life, mistakes happen. Use a seam ripper when necessary. Strive for perfection, learn from your mistakes, but also forgive yourself for not being perfect. The Amish place a deliberate mistake in a quilt as a "humility block" because they believe only God is perfect.

PRESSING

Remember the purpose of pressing is to make the seam, unit, block, and the quilt top as *flat* as possible. Iron from the right side whenever possible. Follow the pressing arrows given in the directions. If you follow these, most, if not all of your seams will alternate.

TWISTING THE SEAM

Try this trick whenever you have any type of four-patch unit.
It will make the center seam intersection lie flatter.

Step 1: Before pressing the last seam on a four-patch, grasp the seam with both hands about an inch from the center seam. Twist in opposite directions, opening up a few threads in the seam.

Step 2: Press one seam in one direction, and the other seam in the opposite direction. In the center you will see a tiny four-patch appear, and the center now lies very flat.

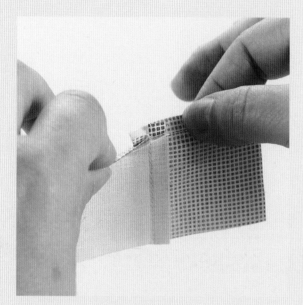

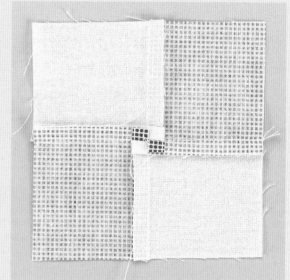

BORDERS

We often make adding borders to a quilt more difficult than it needs to be. Simply cut the strips designated for the borders and piece them as needed. Some people prefer to piece the borders on the diagonal, but the print can also be matched with a straight seam. Choose which method works best for *your* project.

Place the border strips on top of the quilt to measure the length or width of the quilt *through the middle*. Always measure with two border strips together so the borders are guaranteed to be the same length. Crease the border strips at the proper length, but cut an extra inch longer for leeway. Pin the borders to the quilt and sew.

BATTING

The type of batting you use is a personal choice. Cotton batting will give you a flat, traditional look and will shrink a bit when you wash the quilt, giving it a slightly puckered look. Cotton batting is more difficult to hand-quilt, but it will machine-quilt nicely, because the layers of the quilt will not shift readily.

Polyester batting has a bit more loft (puffiness) than a cotton batt and is easier to hand-quilt, but is more slippery, which can cause shifting when machine quilting. Combination poly-and-cotton battings can give you the best qualities of both and are a good choice for hand and machine quilting.

QUILTING

Some of the quilts in this book were hand-quilted, others machine-quilted on a sewing machine, and still others sent out to a long-arm quilter. Regardless of the quilting method used, a short description of how each was quilted can be found at the end of the patterns. Feel free to use these ideas, or create your own quilting designs.

BINDING

Each pattern will suggest bias or straight-of-grain binding, and either single or double binding. Generally, I use double bias or double straight-of-grain binding for any straight edges, and single, bias binding for curved edges.

Step 1: To cut bias binding, trim off the selvages and trim both the bottom and top edges of the fabric chosen for the binding. Using the 45-degree line on your long ruler, align it with the edge of the fabric and cut off the corner at a 45-degree angle. The fabric should be opened, cutting a single layer.

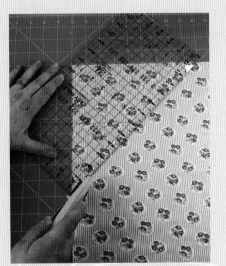

Step 2: Set the corner aside for another use, and cut binding strips from the remainder of the fabric, folding the fabric along the cut edge as needed to shorten the cut.

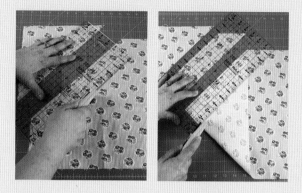

Step 3: After the strips have been cut, join the angled ends exactly as shown. Sew from the "V" at the top of the strip to the "V" at the bottom of the strip (the seam allowance does not have to be ¼"). Join all the strips in this manner to make a continuous binding strip. Press the seams open.

Step 4: To make a double binding, fold the binding in half, wrong sides together, and press.

MITERING CORNERS ON BINDING

Step 1: When the quilting is completed, baste a scant ¼" around the perimeter of the quilt to prevent the layers from shifting while the binding is being sewn on. This prevents the edge from stretching. Leave the excess batting and backing in place until after the binding is sewn on, so you can trim off the exact amount needed to completely fill the binding.

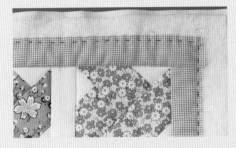

Step 2: Begin sewing the binding to the quilt in the middle of one side, matching the raw edges of the binding to the raw edge of the quilt top. Leave a 6" to 8" tail at the beginning.

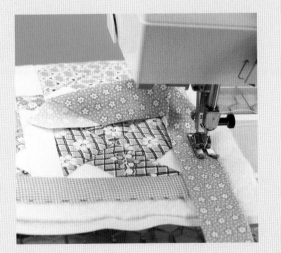

Step 3: To miter a corner, stitch to within a *seam's allowance* from the corner, stop and backstitch.

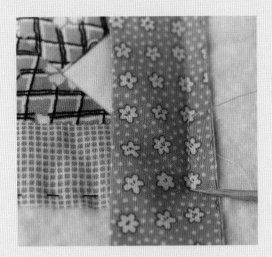

Step 4: Remove the quilt from under the presser foot and trim the threads. Turn the quilt 90 degrees, and pull the binding straight up, forming a 45-degree angle at the corner.

Step 5: Fold the binding back down, with the fold on the previously stitched edge of the quilt. Begin stitching at the fold. This will build in enough extra binding to turn the corner.

Step 6: For corners that are not square (such as on a table runner), stitch the first edge, stop a seam allowance from the corner, and remove the quilt from under the presser foot. Pull the binding straight up, then fold it back down along the next edge. The fold should now come right to the corner of the quilt. It will not align with the previous edge as in a square corner, but rather at right angles to the next edge. Begin stitching at the previous edge.

BINDING A SCALLOPED OR CURVED EDGE

Do not cut on the marked line! Quilt, then before binding, hand-baste along the marked line to keep the layers from shifting when the binding is attached.

A bias binding is a must for binding curved edges. Cut a 1¼" single-bias binding. (Refer to page 11-12 for detailed instructions on preparing binding.)

Step 1: With raw edges of binding aligned with the marked line on your quilt, begin sewing a ¼" seam. Stitch to the base of the "V", stop with the needle down and lift the presser foot.

Step 2: Pivot the quilt and binding around the needle. Put the presser foot down and begin stitching out of the "V", taking care not to stitch any pleats into the binding.

Step 3: Continue around the quilt in this manner, easing the binding around the curves and pivoting at the inside of the "V".

Step 4: Trim the seam allowance an even ¼", turn to the backside and stitch down by hand with matching thread, covering the stitching line. At the "V", the binding will just fold over upon itself making a little pleat.

"PERFECT FIT" BINDING

Step 1: When you are within 8"-10" of where you began binding, stop stitching. Remove the quilt from under the presser foot and trim the threads.

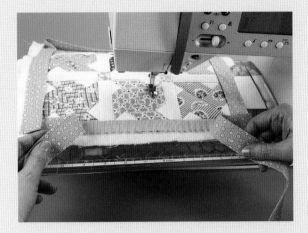

Step 2: On a flat surface, have the binding ends meet in the center of that unstitched area, leaving a scant ¼" between them. Fold the ends over and crease them where they almost meet.

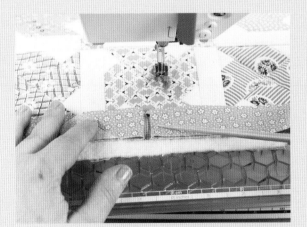

Step 3: Cut one end off at the fold. Then, using the end you have just cut off (open it, if it is a double binding), use it to measure a binding's width away from the fold. Cut off the second end at that measurement.

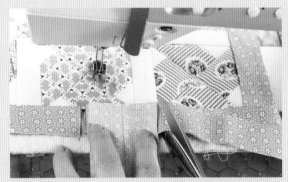

Step 4: Join the ends at right angles with right sides together. Stitch a diagonal seam. Check if the seam is sewn correctly before trimming it to a ¼" seam allowance. Finger press the seam open, and reposition the binding on the quilt.

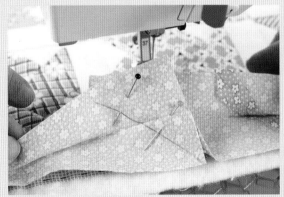

Step 5: Finish stitching the binding to the edge of the quilt.

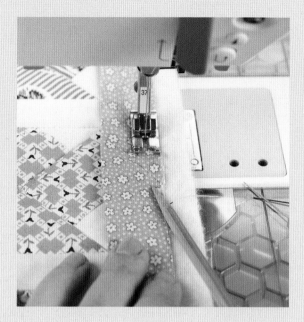

Step 6: Trim the excess batting and backing. On the top side of the quilt, press the binding away from the edge of the quilt to make it easier to stitch on the back side.

Step 7: On the backside of the quilt, fold the binding over the edge so it covers the stitching line. Hand-or machine-sew the binding in place with matching thread.

Tips

- *Use appliqué sharps to hand-stitch the binding. These long, thin needles designed for this type of stitching.*

- *When stitching the binding down by hand, keep the body of the quilt away from you holding only the binding edge. You'll find it easier to stitch.*

- *Use binding clips instead of stick pins to hold the binding edge down for sewing. This is simply to avoid poking yourself!*

QUILT LABELS

Your quilts are your legacy—sign them! A label should include the following:

• Quilt recipient

• Quilt maker

• Date of completion/presentation

• Where the quilt was made

• Special occasion or story

You can purchase fabric labels or create your own. Sew or appliqué the label to the quilt either before or after the quilt is completed.

FREEZER PAPER APPLIQUÉ

The patterns given in this book are reversed for tracing purposes. Trace the shapes on the dull side of the freezer paper.

Note: You can re-use the freezer paper several times.

Step 1: Cut out the shapes on the marked line. Iron the shapes to the wrong side of the fabrics chosen for the appliqué, leaving at least ¾" between the shapes.

Step 2: Cut out the shapes adding a scant ¼" seam allowance. Clip any inside curves.

Step 3: With equal parts liquid starch and water mixture (or spray starch) and a cotton swab, wet the seam allowance of the appliqué piece. Using the tip of the iron, press the seam allowance over the edge of the freezer paper. Once the edge is well-pressed, remove the freezer paper and iron from the right side.

Step 4: Baste in place on the background square either with needle and thread, or Roxanne's Glue Baste-It.

Step 5: Appliqué down by hand or machine zigzag with matching or invisible thread. You might also use black thread and a buttonhole stitch (machine) or black floss (hand).

FUSIBLE APPLIQUÉ

Step 1: Trace the reversed pattern on the paper side of fusible web. Leave a bit of space between each appliqué pattern.

Step 2: Cut out, leaving a small excess of paper around the appliqué. For a softer appliqué, cut out the center of the appliqué shape, leaving at least a ¼" margin inside the shape. Iron to the wrong side of the fabrics chosen for the appliqué, following the manufacturer's instructions for fusing.

Step 3: Cut out on the marked line, then peel off the paper backing. Position the appliqué shape in place on the background fabric and fuse in place, following the manufacturer's directions.

Step 4: By machine or hand, buttonhole stitch around the shapes with matching or invisible thread.

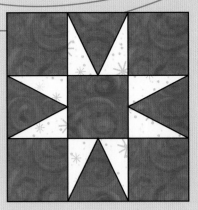

January
FROSTY MORNING

FROSTY MORNING; 54½" x 66½"; 9" blocks; pieced by the author; quilted by Barb Simons of Stone Ridge Quilting, Enderlin, ND.

The crispness of a frosty morning, the clear blue sky, and the magic sparkling tendrils of hoarfrost blanketing every surface. A perfect morning to wrap up in a quilt and sip a cup of coffee, tea, or hot chocolate!

FABRIC REQUIREMENTS

- ⁀ Blue batik swirl fabric: 4 yd.
- ⁀ White/silver snowflake fabric: 1½ yd.
- ⁀ Batting: Twin size
- ⁀ Backing: 3½ yd.

SUGGESTED TOOLS

See Tool Tutorials on pages 118–123.

- ⁀ Tri-Recs
- ⁀ Companion Angle

Frosty Morning Mocha Mix

½ cup powdered coffee creamer
¼ cup sugar
1 tbsp. baking cocoa
5 tsp. instant coffee

Mix well. Use three heaping teaspoons for a small mug, or to taste.

CUTTING DIRECTIONS FOR STAR BLOCKS (Make 20)

From	Cut	To Yield
Blue batik	14—3½" x 42" strips	100—3½" x 3½" squares
		80—Tri triangles (cut with the Tri tool)
White-and-silver print	5—3½" x 42" strips	80 *pairs* of Recs triangles (cut with the Recs tool)

ASSEMBLING THE STAR BLOCKS (Make 20)

Step 1: Sew a white Recs triangle to the right edge of a blue Tri triangle, matching the *magic angle* at the bottom of the unit (see page 118 for tool tutorial). Press toward the white triangle. Repeat to make 80 units.

Step 2: Sew the remaining Recs triangle from the pair to the left side of the unit from step 1, matching the magic angle as before. Press toward the white triangle. Make 80 Tri-Recs units. At this point the Tri-Recs unit should measure 3½" x 3½".

Step 3: Using five 3½" x 3½" blue squares and four Tri-Recs units from step 2, make 20 blocks as shown. Press toward the blue squares. At this point the blocks should measure 9½" x 9½".

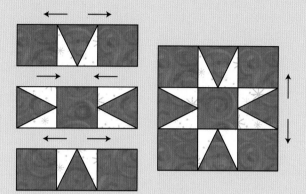

CUTTING DIRECTIONS FOR CHAIN BLOCKS (Full and half)

From	Cut	To Yield
Blue batik	8—3½" x 42" strips	82—3½" x 3½" squares
	10—2" x 42" strips	Four-patches
	5—2¾" x 42" strips	58 Companion Angle* triangles
	2¼" bias strips	260" of bias binding
White-and-silver print	3—3½" x 42" strips	30—3½" x 3½" squares
	10—2" x 42" strips	Four-patches

If not using Companion Angle, cut 15—5¾" x 5¾" squares; cut twice on the diagonal.

ASSEMBLING THE CHAIN BLOCKS (Make 12)

Step 1: Sew the 2" × 42" blue strips together with the 2" × 42" white strips to make ten strip sets. Press toward the blue strips.

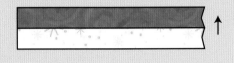

Step 2: Cut the strip sets from step 1 into 196 units 2" wide.

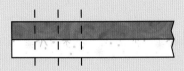

Step 3: Sew together the units from step 2 into 98 four-patch units. Twist the center seam to open (see page 10 for more on this technique). Press.

Step 4: Sew together four 3½" × 3½" blue squares, one 3½" × 3½" white square, and four four-patch units to make a block. Press the seams toward the blue squares. At this point the block should measure 9½" × 9½". Make 12 chain blocks.

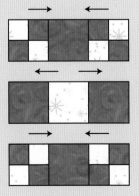
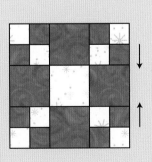

Step 5: Sew together two 3½" × 3½" blue squares, one 3½" × 3½" white square, three four-patch units, and three blue triangles to make a large, pieced setting triangle. Press toward the blue squares, and the triangles are pressed as shown.

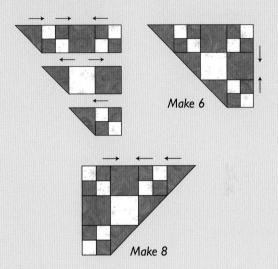

Make 6

Make 8

Step 6: For the corner triangles, sew together one white 3½" × 3½" square, one blue 3½" × 3½" square, two four-patch units, and four blue triangles. Press toward the blue squares and triangles.

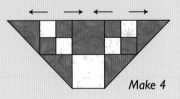

Make 4

Step 7: Cut the remaining two blue 3½" × 3½" squares once on the diagonal to make triangles for the tip of the pieced corner triangles. Press toward the triangle. Make four corner triangles.

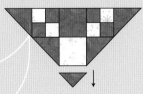

ASSEMBLING THE QUILT

Step 1: Arrange the blocks in diagonal rows, alternating the star blocks and the chain blocks. Add the pieced setting triangles along the outside edges. Refer to the quilt assembly diagram on opposite page.

Step 2: Sew the blocks together in rows, pinning and matching seam intersections, and pressing toward the chain blocks and setting triangles.

Step 3: Sew the rows together, pinning and matching seam intersections. Press the seams all in one direction.

Note: If needed, the edges of the quilt can be straightened. Just be careful to leave at least a ¼" seam allowance from the corners of the units.

FINISHING THE QUILT

Step 1: Piece a backing that is at least 3" larger all around than the quilt top. Trim the batting to the same size as the backing. Layer with the backing wrong side up, the batting, then the quilt top right side up. Baste.

Step 2: The quilt shown was machine-quilted in a swirled snowflake pattern in silver thread.

Step 3: Before binding, hand-baste a scant ¼" from the edge of the quilt to keep the layers from shifting while binding.

BINDING

Step 1: Join the 2¼" bias strips with diagonal seams pressed open. Press the binding in half, wrong sides together. (See page 11 for more instruction on preparing a bias binding.)

Step 2: Sew the binding to the quilt with a ¼" seam allowance, mitering the corners. (See page 13 for more instruction on mitering corners.)

Step 3: Join the binding ends with the "Perfect Fit" binding technique shown on page 15.

Step 4: Trim the excess batting and backing, turn the binding to the back side and stitch down by hand with matching thread.

Create, sign, and attach a label, and your quilt is ready for those frosty mornings in January!

Frosty Morning quilt assembly

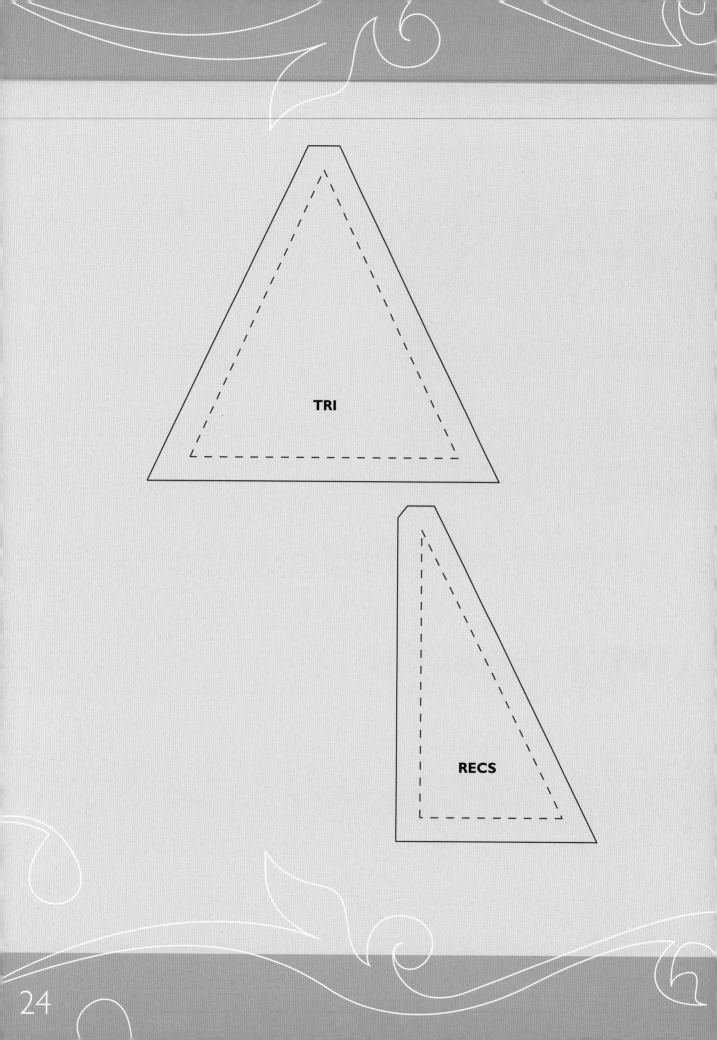

TRI

RECS

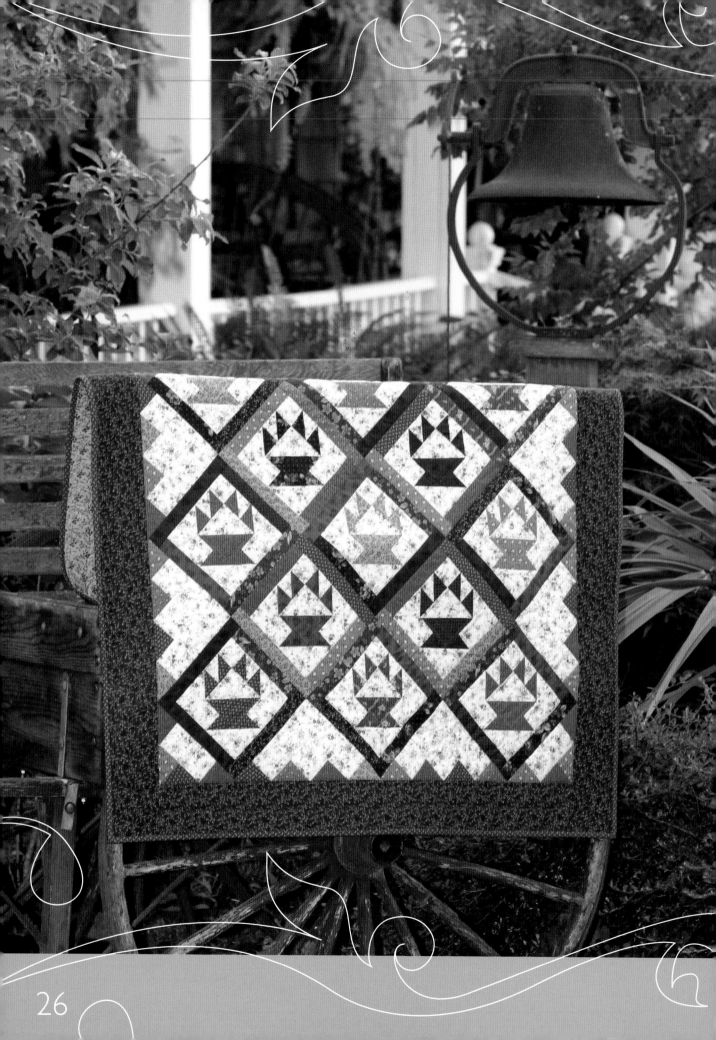

February

CHOCOLATE RASPBERRY TRUFFLE

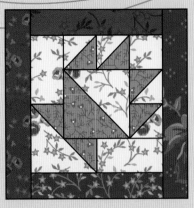

CHOCOLATE RASPBERRY TRUFFLE; 41" × 52"; 8" blocks; made by the author.

February is a month for sweethearts, which brings to mind roses and chocolates. With pink and red prints symbolizing roses for your sweetheart, and chocolate prints for the sweets we love, create this no-calorie, fat-free CHOCOLATE RASPBERRY TRUFFLE quilt!

> Winter is the time for comfort, for good food and warmth, for the touch of a friendly hand and for a talk beside the fire; it is the time for home.
>
> — Edith Sitwell

FABRIC REQUIREMENTS

- Cream floral background: 1¼ yd.
- Assorted pink prints: 6 fat quarters
- Assorted brown prints: 3 fat quarters
- Brown print for border: ⅔ yd.
- Pink print for binding: ⅜ yd.
- Backing: 2⅔ yd.
- Batting: Crib size

SUGGESTED TOOLS

See Tool Tutorials on pages 118–123.

- Easy Angle
- Companion Angle

CUTTING DIRECTIONS FOR BLOCKS

From	Cut	To Yield
Background fabric	2—3½" × 42" strips	36—3½" Easy Angle triangles*
	7—2" × 42" strips*	72—2" Easy Angle triangles*
		36—2" × 3½" rectangles
		18—2" × 2" squares
Each pink fabric	1—3½" × 21" strip	2—3½" Easy Angle triangles*
	1—2" × 21" strip	12—2" Easy Angle triangles*
	2—1½" × 21" strips	2—1½" × 8½" rectangles
		2—1½" × 6½" rectangles
Each brown fabric	1—3½" × 21" strip	2—3½" Easy Angle triangles*
	1—2" × 21" strip*	12—2" Easy Angle triangles*
	7—1½" × 21" strips	8—1½" × 8½" rectangles
		8—1½" × 6½" rectangles

If not using Easy Angle, cut 3⅞" and 2⅜" squares, respectively. Cut once on the diagonal.

ASSEMBLING THE BASKET BLOCKS (Make 12 pink and 6 brown)

Step 1: Match either a large or small background triangles right sides together with either a pink or brown triangle. From each fabric sew eight matching small and two matching large triangle squares together. Press toward the darker fabric. Trim the dog-ears. (There will be some small brown and pink triangles left over for step 6.)

Make 2   Make 8

Step 2: Sew matching small triangle squares together in A and B pairs as shown. Press.

A   B

Step 3: Sew the A sets of triangle squares from step 2 to the left side of the matching large triangle squares. Press. Repeat for each of the 18 basket blocks.

Step 4: Sew a background square to the left side of the B-triangle squares from step 2. Press towards the square. Repeat for each of the B-triangle squares.

Step 5: Sew the step 4 units to the top of the step 3 units. Press.

Step 6: Sew a matching pair of small pink or brown triangles to the 2" x 3½" background rectangles as shown. Make two A's and B's of each print. Trim the dog-ears. Press.

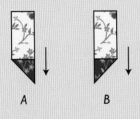

A   B

Step 7: Sew the step 6 units to adjacent sides of the basket blocks. Trim dog-ears. Press.

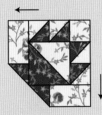

Step 8: Sew a background triangle to the bottom of the block. Press. At this point the blocks should measure 6½" x 6½".

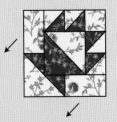

Note: If your blocks measure less than 6½" x 6½", trim the sashing strips in the next two steps to fit your blocks.

SASHING THE BLOCKS

Step 1: Using two different 1½" x 6½" pink sashings, sew them to opposite sides of the brown basket blocks. Press toward the sashing.

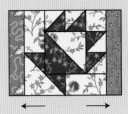

Step 2: Using different 1½" x 8½" pink sashings, sew to the remaining sides of the brown basket blocks. Press toward the sashing.

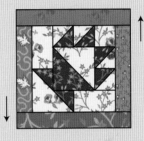

Step 3: Using different 1½" x 6½" brown sashings, sew to opposite sides of the pink basket blocks. Press toward the sashing.

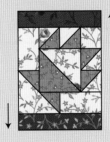

Note: The sashings are sewn on opposite sides from the brown basket blocks.

Step 4: Using different 1½" x 8½" brown sashings, sew to the remaining sides of the pink basket blocks. Press toward the sashing.

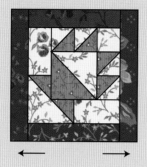

CUTTING SETTING TRIANGLES, BORDERS AND BINDING

From	Cut	To Yield
Background fabric	2—4½" x 42" strips	10—4½" x 4½" squares
	2—2½" x 42" strips	28—2½" x 2½" squares
Each pink fabric	2—2" x 21" strips	10—Companion Angle triangles*
Brown border fabric	5—4" x 42" strips	Border
Pink binding fabric	5—2¼" x 42" strips	Binding

If not using Companion Angle, cut three 4¼" x 4¼" squares from each fabric. Cut the squares twice on the diagonal to yield twelve triangles. You will have some left over.

ASSEMBLING THE SETTING TRIANGLES

Step 1: Sew a pink triangle to the right side of the 2½" x 2½" background square. Press toward the triangle. Repeat for each of the background squares.

Step 2: Sew a different pink triangle to the left side of the step 1 units. Press toward the triangles. (You will have some triangles left over.)

Step 3: Sew a step 2 unit to the right side of a 4½" x 4½" background square. Repeat to make a total of ten units. Press toward the background square.

Step 4: Sew a step 2 unit to the left side of the step 3 unit. Press. Repeat to make a total of ten units.

Step 5: Using two of the step 2 units, sew together to make a corner triangle. Repeat to make four corner triangles. Press the seam open.

ASSEMBLING THE QUILT TOP

Step 1: Arrange the setting triangles and the pink and brown blocks in diagonal rows as shown. Sew the blocks together in rows. Press the seams toward the brown sashing.

Step 2: Sew the rows together, pinning and matching seam allowances. Press the row seams all one direction.

Step 3: Trim the edges even if necessary, *leaving at least ¼" seam allowance from the corners of the brown sashing.*

BORDERS

Step 1: Measure the quilt width through the center of the quilt. Trim two 4" x 42" brown borders to this length. Sew to the top and bottom of the quilt, pressing the seams toward the borders. See page 11 for more instruction on adding borders.

Step 2: Measure the quilt length through the center of the quilt. Diagonally piece the remaining three border strips, then trim two borders the length of the quilt. Sew to the sides of the quilt, pressing the seams toward the borders just added.

FINISHING THE QUILT

Step 1: Piece the backing, and trim the excess, allowing at least 2" extra on all sides of the quilt top. Trim the batting to the same size as the backing. Layer the backing wrong side up, then the batting, and lastly the quilt top, right side up. Baste.

Step 2: Quilt as desired. The quilt shown was machine-quilted in the ditch around each of the blocks and the frames. Hand-quilting was added inside the blocks. A four-petaled flower was quilted in the large setting triangles and a design was quilted in the border.

Step 3: Before binding, hand-baste a scant ¼" from the edge of the quilt to hold the layers together and prevent shifting while the binding is being sewn on.

BINDING

Step 1: Prepare the binding by sewing together the pink 2¼" x 42" binding lengths with diagonal seams pressed open. Press the binding in half the long way, with the right side out. (See page 11 for more instruction on preparing binding.)

Step 2: Sew the binding to the quilt with a ¼" seam, mitering the corners. (See page 13 for mitering corners.)

Step 3: Join the binding ends with a "Perfect Fit" ending. (See page 15 for more instruction on ending the binding.)

Sign your quilt and enjoy!

Chocolate Raspberry Truffle quilt assembly

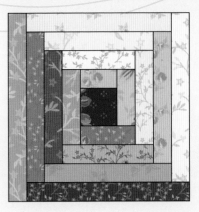

March
SWEET DELIGHTS

SWEET DELIGHTS; 93" x 106"; 10" blocks; pieced by the author; quilted by Lois Sather of Country Quilting, Madison, MN.

In Oregon, spring arrives in early March. Buds are popping out everywhere; early spring flowers are starting to bloom. Spend a pleasant spring afternoon with an elegant quilt, a good book, and a cup of tea.

Spring Herbal Tea

*1 cup fresh mint, lemon balm, or lemon verbena
or ¼ cup fresh lemon thyme plus 3 leaves spearmint*
1 quart boiling water

Put herbs in a teapot and add boiling water. Let steep three minutes before serving.

FABRIC REQUIREMENTS

- Light prints: 16 fat quarters or scraps totaling at least 4 yd.
- Dark prints: 19 fat quarters or scraps totaling at least 5 yd.
- Block center: 1 fat quarter
- Setting triangles and border: 4⅓ yd.
- Accent border and binding: 1⅜ yd.
- Batting: King size
- Backing: 8¼ yd.

SUGGESTED TOOLS

See Tool Tutorials on pages 118–123.

- Flip-n-Set
- Easy Scallop

CUTTING DIRECTIONS FOR LOG CABIN BLOCKS

From	Cut	To Yield
Block center fabric	7—2½" x 21" strips	50—2½" x 2½" squares
Each dark fat quarter	8—1½" x 21" strips or total of 152—1½" x 21" strips	Cut 50 each— 1½" x 10½" 1½" x 9½" 1½" x 8½" 1½" x 7½" 1½" x 6½" 1½" x 5½" 1½" x 4½" 1½" x 3½" Cut largest sizes first.
Each light fat quarter	8—1½" x 21" strips or total of 128—1½" x 21" strips	Cut 50 each— 1½" x 9½" 1½" x 8½" 1½" x 7½" 1½" x 6½" 1½" x 5½" 1½" x 4½" 1½" x 3½" 1½" x 2½" Cut largest sizes first.

LOG CABIN BLOCK ASSEMBLY

Step 1: Starting with a block center and a light 1½" x 2½" rectangle, sew together and press toward the light rectangle.

Step 2: Turn the block a quarter-turn to the left (or counterclockwise) and sew a light 1½" x 3½" rectangle. Press toward the rectangle.

Step 3: Turn the block a quarter turn to the left (or counterclockwise) and add a dark 1½" x 3½" rectangle. Press toward the rectangle.

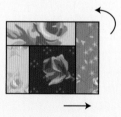

Step 4: Turn the block a quarter turn to the left (or counterclockwise) and add a dark 1½" x 4½" rectangle. Press toward the rectangle.

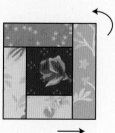

Step 5: Continue in this manner, turning counterclockwise and sewing two dark rectangles and two light rectangles to adjacent sides of the block, pressing after each addition. Make 50 blocks. At this point the blocks should measure 10½" x 10½".

Note: The rectangles have been cut the right length. If they don't fit properly, you will need to adjust your seam allowance to sew an accurate ¼" seam.

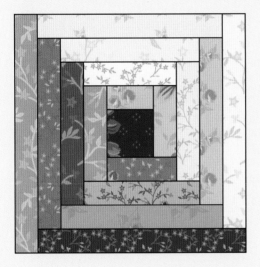

CUTTING THE SETTING TRIANGLES

Step 1: From the setting triangles and border fabric, cut four 8" x 42" strips.* Open up the fabric strips and cut a total of sixteen setting triangles using Flip-n-Set.

Step 2: Cut one strip 9" wide. From that strip cut two 9" squares, cut once on the diagonal for corner triangles.

Step 3: Trim the remainder of the strip to 8", and cut two more setting triangles with Flip-n-Set for a total of 18 setting triangles.

* If not using Flip-n-Set, cut five 15½" squares. Cut each square twice on the diagonal for twenty setting triangles. You will only need eighteen setting triangles.

ASSEMBLING THE QUILT

Step 1: Arrange the blocks in diagonal rows as shown. Use the setting triangles along the edges and the corner triangles at the corners.

Step 2: Sew the blocks together in diagonal rows, alternating the direction the seams are pressed in each row.

Step 3: Sew the rows together, matching and pinning seam intersections. Press all the row seams in one direction.

Tip

Setting triangles are cut slightly over-sized so you can straighten the edges of the quilt. To do this, lay a large square (or Flip-n-Set) over one corner. Mark a square corner with chalk or pencil. Repeat on each of the corners. Using a long ruler, connect the lines at the corners. Do not cut off the corners of the log cabin blocks! Trim the quilt to within ¼" or more from the corners of the blocks. After you are satisfied the marks are as straight as can be, trim on the marked lines.

BORDERS

Step 1: From the accent border fabric, cut a total of nine 1½" x 42" strips. Join the strips with diagonal seams pressed open.

Step 2: Measure the quilt through the width. Cut two borders to this length and sew to the top and bottom of the quilt. Press the seams toward the borders. Repeat for the side borders. (See page 11 for more instruction on adding borders.)

Step 3: From the outer border and setting triangle fabric, cut four 10½"-wide borders the length of the remaining fabric (or as wide as your fabric will allow).

Step 4: Measure the width of your quilt. Trim two borders to this measurement and sew to the top and bottom of your quilt. Press toward the borders just added. Repeat for the side borders. Press toward the borders just added.

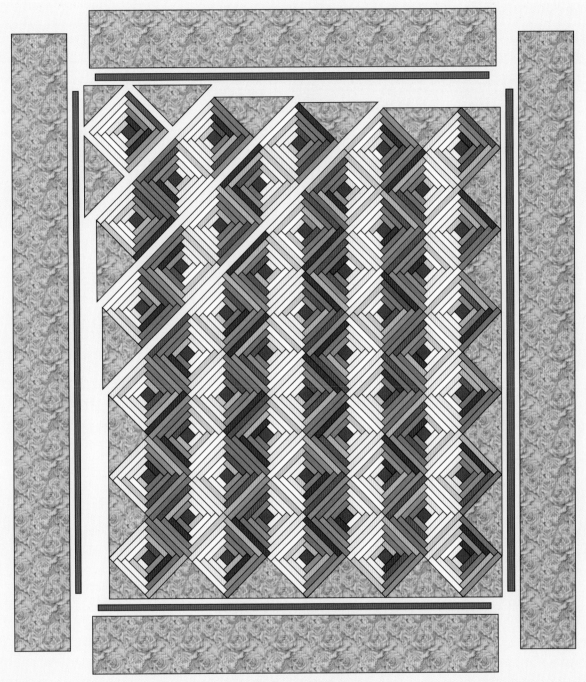

Sweet Delights quilt assembly

FINISHING THE QUILT

Step 1: Cut the backing fabric into three equal lengths and sew together to make the backing. Trim the batting to the same size as the backing.

Step 2: Layer the backing wrong side up, the batting, and then the quilt top right side up. Baste.

Step 3: Quilt as desired. The quilt shown was machine-quilted with feathers down the length of the quilt on the dark side of the blocks, and in the ditch down the center on the light side of the blocks. Feathers were also quilted in the border.

MARKING A SCALLOPED BORDER

Step 1: The top and bottom borders were marked using Easy Scallop set at a 10¼" scallop. The sides were marked with a 10½" scallop. The corners were rounded. Remember to mark from the corners to the center, adjusting the center one or two scallops as needed. See page 122 for more instructions on marking a scalloped edge.

Step 2: Baste on the marked scallop line, but *do not* cut on that line. The basting will hold the layers together and prevent shifting while the binding is being sewn on.

BINDING

Step 1: From the accent and binding fabric, trim off the selvages, then cut a 45-degree corner off the opened fabric. Set the corner aside for another project. Cut 1¼" bias strips from the remainder of the fabric to total approximately 500". (See page 11 for more instruction on cutting bias binding.) Join the bias binding strips with diagonal seams pressed open.

Step 2: Matching the binding edge to the marked line, sew a ¼" seam allowance, stopping and pivoting at the "V." (See page 14 for more instruction on binding a scalloped edge.)

Step 3: Following the instructions on pages 15–16, join the binding ends with the "Perfect Fit" technique.

Step 4: Trim excess batting and backing, turn to the back side and stitch down with matching thread. There is no need to clip in the "V."

Sign and date!

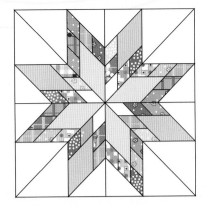

April
DAFFODIL STARS

Daffodil Stars; 82" × 102"; 18½" blocks; quilted by the author.

Daffodil Stars is a circa 1930s quilt top I purchased years ago, and recently hand-quilted. With the soft colors of butter yellow and sweet lavender, it is the perfect spring quilt to brighten any room and lift your spirits!

The piecing directions are updated for use with cutting tools, but diamond templates are also provided if you prefer an alternate method. There are no set-in seams in piecing this wonderful star block, just easy-to-assemble triangle and diamond units.

*I wandered lonely as a cloud
That floats on high o'er vales and hills,
When all at once I saw a crowd,
A host, of golden daffodils*

— William Wordsworth

FABRIC REQUIREMENTS

- ∽ Vintage white: 4 yd.
- ∽ Lavender solid: 2 yd.
- ∽ Yellow solid: 2½ yd.
- ∽ Variety of prints: 12 fat quarters
- ∽ Backing: 7⅓ yd.
- ∽ Batting: Queen size

SUGGESTED TOOLS

See Tool Tutorials on pages 118–123.

- ∽ Easy Angle (6½" size)
- ∽ 45-Degree Diamond

CUTTING DIRECTIONS

From	Cut	To Yield
Vintage white	14—6" × 42" strips	160—6" Easy Angle triangles*
	10—4¼" × 42" strips	160—4¼" Easy Angle triangles*
	6—1¾" × 42" strips	80 small diamonds**
Lavender solid	10—3" × 42" strips	80 large diamonds**
	2—2" × 42" strips	30—2" × 2" cornerstones
	2¼" bias strips	400" of bias binding
Yellow solid	10—3" × 42" strips	80 large diamonds**
	25—2" × 42" strips	49—2" × 19" sashes
Variety of prints	103—1¾" × 21" strips	720 small diamonds**

* If not using Easy Angle, cut 80—6⅜" and 4⅝" squares respectively; cut once on the diagonal.

** If not using the 45-Degree Diamond tool, use the templates on page 46.

ASSEMBLING THE STAR BLOCKS (Make 20)

Note: To prevent stretching the units, please handle carefully and avoid steam until the final pressing.

Step 1: Using a variety of small diamonds, sew 160 pairs *exactly as shown*. Press the seam toward the left.

Step 2: Sew the pairs to the *left* side of the lavender and yellow large diamonds. Press toward the large diamonds.

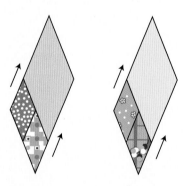

Step 3: Sew three small print diamonds together to make a total of 80 units *exactly as shown*. Press the seams.

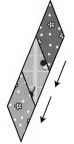

Step 4: Sew the units from step 3 to the adjacent side of the large yellow diamonds from step 2. Press toward the small diamonds. Make 80 large yellow diamonds.

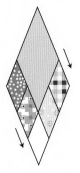

Step 5: Sew two small print diamonds and one small white diamond together to make a total of 80 units *exactly as shown*. Press the seams toward the white diamonds.

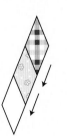

Step 6: Sew the step 5 units to the adjacent side of the large lavender diamonds from step 2. Press the seams towards the small diamonds. Make 80 large lavender diamonds.

Step 7: Sew a small white triangle to the left side of the lavender diamond. Press toward the lavender diamond. Repeat to make a total of 80 units.

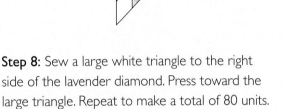

Step 8: Sew a large white triangle to the right side of the lavender diamond. Press toward the large triangle. Repeat to make a total of 80 units.

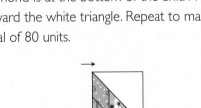

Step 9: Sew a small white triangle to the right side of the yellow diamond units from step 4. Note that you are sewing the white triangle to the small diamonds, and the large yellow diamond is at the bottom of the unit. Press toward the white triangle. Repeat to make a total of 80 units.

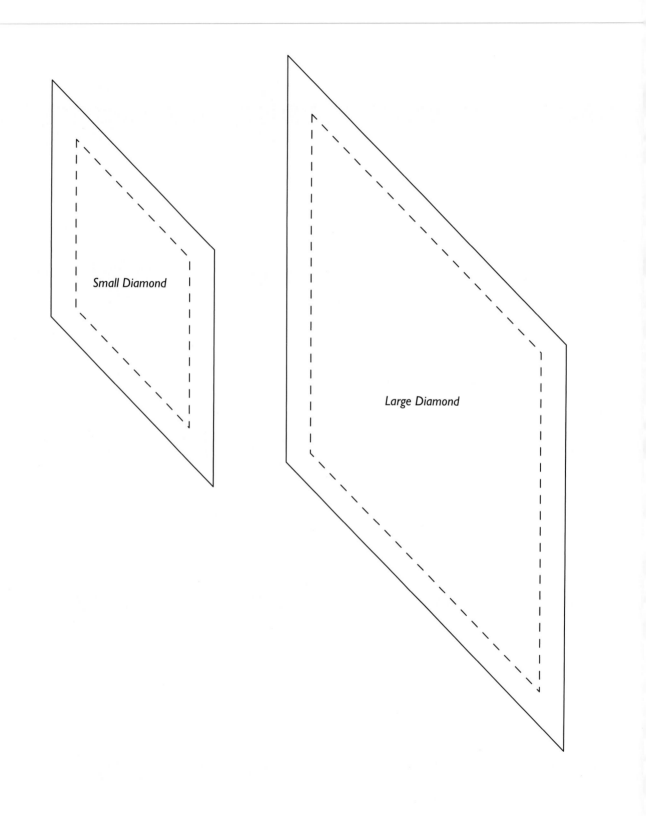

Small Diamond

Large Diamond

Step 10: Sew a large white triangle to the left side of the units from step 9. Press the seam toward the small diamonds. Make a total of 80 units.

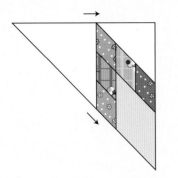

Step 11: Sew one yellow diamond unit and one lavender diamond unit together to make a square. All the seams should alternate. Press the seam to the right. Repeat to make a total of 80 units.

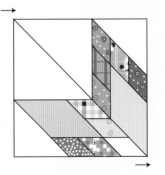

Step 12: Sew the step 11 units together in pairs. Press the seam to the right. Make 40 units.

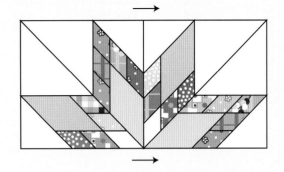

Step 13: Pinning and matching centers, sew two units from step 12 together to make a block. Twist the center seam to open so the seam allowances spin around the center. Press. Repeat to make a total of 20 blocks. At this point the blocks should measure 19".

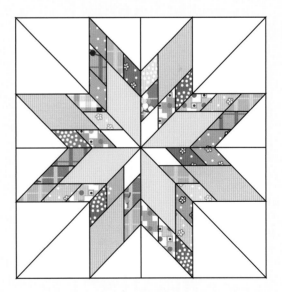

ASSEMBLING THE QUILT

Step 1: Arrange the blocks in five rows of four blocks. Sew yellow sashing strips between the blocks and on both ends of the rows. Press toward the sashing strips. Make five rows.

Step 2: Sew four yellow sashings and five lavender cornerstones together to make a horizontal sashing row. Press toward the sashings. Make a total of six horizontal sashing rows.

Step 3: Sew the rows from step 1 and step 2 together, pinning and matching seam intersections. Press the seams toward the sashings.

FINISHING THE QUILT

Step 1: Piece a backing at least 4" larger on all sides than the quilt top. Trim the batting to the same size as the backing.

Step 2: Layer the backing wrong side up, the batting, and then the quilt top right side up and baste together.

Step 3: Quilt as desired. The quilt shown was hand-quilted a scant ¼" inside each of the large and small diamonds, squares, and triangles. A four-petal flower motif was stitched in the block corners and a half motif was stitched in the triangles. A small cable design was stitched in the sashing.

Step 4: Before binding, hand-baste a scant ¼" from the edge of the quilt to hold the layers together.

BINDING

Step 1: Join the 2¼" lavender solid bias binding strips with diagonal seams pressed open to make a binding at least 400". (See page 11 for more instruction on cutting a bias binding.)

Step 2: Fold the binding in half, wrong sides together, and press to make a double bias binding.

Step 3: Sew the binding to the quilt with a ¼" seam allowance, mitering the corners. (See page 13 for more instruction on mitering corners.)

Step 4: Join the binding ends with the "Perfect Fit" binding technique shown on pages 15–16.

Step 5: Trim any excess batting and backing, turn the binding to the wrong side, and stitch down by hand with matching thread.

Sign and date your Daffodil Stars quilt!

DAFFODIL STARS quilt assembly

May
LAVENDER GATHERING BASKETS

Lavender Gathering Baskets; 18½" × 27½"; pieced, embroidered, and quilted by the author.

Throughout the summer months at Lavender Hill Farm, friends and visitors alike are greeted at the door with an invitation to take home a bouquet of lovely scented flowers. Garden snips and gathering baskets are provided, and the lucky visitor has the special pleasure of picking lavender from a fragrant hillside. The lavender can be displayed fresh in flower arrangements or dried and used as sachets, brewed in tea, or to decorate a room.

This fanciful quilt brings to mind lovely sprigs of lavender, fresh flowers, and long lazy summer days buzzing with honeybees.

FABRIC REQUIREMENTS

- 6 different lavender-and-pink prints: 1 fat eighth of each
- Cream tone-on-tone: ⅓ yd.
- Green print: ⅜ yd.
- Backing: ⅔ yd.
- Batting: 22" × 31"

ADDITIONAL REQUIREMENTS

- Embroidery floss in dark and medium lavender; dark and medium pink; bright yellow; sage; dark green; and brown.

EMBROIDERED BLOCKS

Step 1: From the cream tone-on-tone, cut two blocks for embroidery larger than needed at 10" x 13". Make a copy of the design on the opposite page to trace using a light box or by taping it to a bright window. With a blue wash-out pen trace the embroidery design onto the right side of the cream tone-on-tone blocks.

Step 2: Refer to the basket design on the opposite page for color placement, and embroider the block using two strands of floss. The flower petals and small leaves are stitched with a lazy daisy stitch. The larger yellow flowers have satin-stitched centers. The basket, larger leaves, and stems are embroidered with an outline stitch. The flower centers and the lilac flowers are French knots.

Lazy daisy   Satin-stitch

Outline stitch   French knots

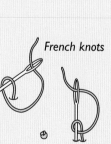

Step 3: After the embroidery is completed, soak the blocks in cold water to remove the blue marks. Dry flat. Iron the blocks face down on a fluffy towel. *Trim the blocks evenly to 8½" x 11½".*

Step 4: From the green print, cut one 2½" x 42" strip. Cut it into eight 2½" x 2½" squares..

Step 5: Mark a diagonal line on the wrong side of each of the 2½" x 2½" green squares. Place a green square over the corner of one of the embroidered blocks and sew on the line. Trim the seam allowance to ¼" and press the seam towards the green triangle. Repeat on each of the corners.

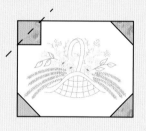

Step 6: From the green print cut three 1" x 42" strips. From those strips cut four 1" x 11½" rectangles, and four 1" x 9½" rectangles. Sew the 1" x 11½" strips to the top and bottom of the two embroidered blocks. Press toward the borders. Sew the 1" x 9½" strips to the sides of the blocks. Press toward the borders.

SASHING AND BORDERS

Step 1: From each of the lavender-and-pink fat eighths, cut two 2" × 21" strips. Cut them into 2" × 10½" strips. Randomly sew the 2" × 10½" strips together into pairs. *Without pressing, and leaving the strip sets folded together,* cut the strip sets into 60—2" wide units.

Step 2: Open up the units from step 1 and arrange them into a row of eight units. Press the seams so that they alternate. Sew the units together. Press the seams all one direction. Repeat to make a total of three units.

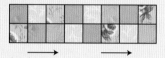

Step 3: Sew a unit to the top of each of the embroidered blocks. Sew one unit to the bottom of one of the blocks. Sew the blocks together as shown in the picture. Press the seams toward the green sashing.

Step 4: In the same manner as in step 2, sew together 18 units to make a side border for the quilt. Make two side borders. Press the seams so they alternate with the seams on the center section of the quilt. Sew to the sides of the quilt. Press the seams toward the center section.

Step 5: Mark the edge of the quilt 3" from each of the corners. Mark a line connecting the marks at each corner. Cut on that line.

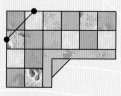

FINISHING THE QUILT

Step 1: Trim the batting and backing several inches larger than the quilt top on all sides. Layer with backing wrong side up, batting, and then the quilt top right side up and baste.

Step 2: Quilt as desired. The quilt shown was machine-quilted in the ditch around the blocks and green sashing, and stitched in the ditch between each of the squares in the border. The embroidered block was hand-quilted in cross-hatching around the basket and flowers, and a few lines of stitching follow the lines of the basket.

Step 3: Before sewing on the binding, hand-baste a scant ¼" from the edge of the quilt to hold all the layers together.

BINDING

Step 1: Cut three 2¼" × 42" strips of green print for binding. Join with diagonal seams pressed open (see page 12 for more instruction). Press the binding in half, wrong sides together, along the length.

Step 2: Sew the binding to the quilt with a ¼" seam, stopping and mitering at each corner. (See page 13 for more instruction on mitering corners.)

Step 3: Join the binding ends using the "Perfect Fit" technique shown on page 15.

Step 4: Trim the excess batting and backing, turn the binding to the back side, and stitch down by hand with matching thread.

Sign and date!

LAVENDER GATHERING BASKETS quilt assembly

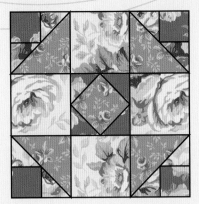

June
WILD ROSES

WILD ROSES; 66" x 84"; 9" blocks; pieced by the author; quilted by Cindy Larson at Country Roads Machine Quilting.

June is a time of wild roses blooming along the winding country roads, bringing with them the promise of summer. This romantic rose quilt is the perfect celebration of early summer and the halcyon days it brings. The quilt was photographed on the split-rail fence that meanders along one side of the drive leading to the house. Judy has trained old-fashioned roses to climb along the fence as a lovely (and fragrant) welcome to her home as you wend your way up to Lavender Hill Farm.

> What though youth gave love and roses,
> Age still leaves us friends and wine.
>
> — *Thomas More*

FABRIC REQUIREMENTS

- Large floral print: 5 yd.
- Green print: ¾ yd.
- Dark rose print: 1½ yd.
- Backing: 5 yd.
- Batting: Twin size

SUGGESTED TOOLS

See Tool Tutorials on pages 118–123.

- Easy Angle
- Easy Scallop

CUTTING DIRECTIONS

From	Cut	To Yield
Large floral	5—9½" x 42" strips	17—9½" x 9½" squares (fussy cut if desired)
	7—3½" x 42" strips	72—3½" x 3½" squares for blocks
	5—2" x 42" strips*	144—Easy Angle triangles*
	4—9½" x 90" strips cut lengthwise	Outer border
Dark rose	8—2" x 42" strips	144—2" x 2" squares
	6—2" x 42" strips	Inner border
	1¼" bias strips	400" of bias binding
Green print	2—3½" x 42" strips	18—3½" x 3½" squares
	4—3½" x 42" strips**	72—Easy Angle triangles**

* If not using Easy Angle, cut 72—2⅜" squares, then cut once on the diagonal.

** If not using Easy Angle, cut 36—3⅞" squares, then cut once on the diagonal.

ASSEMBLING THE BLOCKS (Make 18)

Step 1: Mark a diagonal line on the wrong side of 72—2" x 2" dark rose squares. Place one square over the corner of the green 3½" x 3½" square. Sew on the diagonal line, trim the seam allowance to ¼" and press toward the green square. Repeat on the opposite corner.

Step 2: Sew a 2" x 2" dark rose square on the remaining two corners of the green square from step 1. Trim and press the seams toward the dark rose triangles. At this point the unit should measure 3½" x 3½". Make a total of 18 units.

Step 3: Sew a floral print triangle to the right side of a 2" x 2" dark rose square as shown. Press toward the small triangle. Make 72 units.

Step 4: Sew another floral print triangle to the adjacent edge of the step 3 unit. Press toward the dark rose square. Make 72 units.

Step 5: Sew a large green triangle to the unit from step 4. Press toward the green triangle. At this point the square should measure 3½" × 3½". Make 72 units.

Step 6: Sew four units from step 5, one unit from step 2, and large floral print 3½" × 3½" squares together to make a block. Press as shown. At this point, the block should measure 9½" × 9½". Repeat to make a total of 18 blocks.

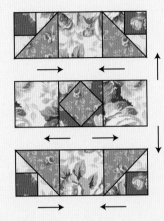

ASSEMBLING THE QUILT

Step 1: Assemble the blocks in rows as shown, alternating the pieced blocks with the large floral print squares. Press the seams toward the large floral print squares. Sew seven rows of five blocks.

Step 2: Sew the rows together, matching and pinning seam intersections. Press the seams all one direction.

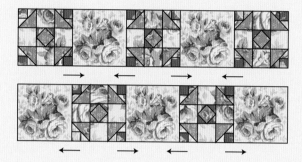

BORDERS

Step 1: Piece, measure, and trim two 2" x 42" dark rose borders to the width of the quilt. Sew to the top and bottom of the quilt. Press toward the borders. (See page 11 for more instruction on adding borders.)

Step 2: Piece, measure, and trim two 2" x 42" dark rose borders to the length of the quilt. Sew to the sides of the quilt. Press toward the borders.

Step 3: Using the large floral 9½" x 90" borders, measure and trim two borders the width of the quilt *plus 5–6" extra to allow for centering the motifs.* Center the motifs, then sew the borders to the top and bottom of the quilt. Press toward the borders just added.

Step 4: Repeat measuring, trimming, and centering to fit the last two borders to the sides of the quilt. Sew to the sides, and press toward the borders.

*W*ILD *R*OSES *quilt assembly*

FINISHING THE QUILT

Step 1: Piece the backing, then trim to 3"–4" larger than the quilt top on all sides. Trim the batting to the same size. Layer backing wrong side up, the batting, then the quilt top right side up. Baste.

Step 2: Quilt as desired. The quilt shown was machine-quilted in the ditch around the squares and triangles in the pieced blocks. The alternate blocks and border were quilted in an all-over stipple, highlighting the floral motif. There was a small scroll stitched in the narrow dark rose inner border.

Step 3: Mark the scalloped borders of the right curvature using Easy Scallop or a lid or plate. The scallops along the top and bottom of the quilt measure 11". The scallops at the sides of the quilt measure 10½". Corners are not marked, but left square. See page 122 for more instruction on marking a scalloped edge.

Step 4: Baste on the marked scallop line to hold the layers together and prevent shifting while the binding is being sewn on. *Do not* trim on the curved edge.

BINDING

Step 1: Sew the dark rose single bias binding strips together with diagonal seams pressed open. See page 11 for preparing a bias binding.

Step 2: Sew the binding to the quilt, aligning the binding with the marked scallop edge, and stitching a ¼" seam. See page 14 for more instruction on binding a scalloped edge.

Step 3: Join the binding ends with the "Perfect Fit" technique shown on page 15.

Step 4: Trim excess batting and backing, turn the binding to the back side of the quilt and stitch down by hand with matching thread.

Sign and date.

July
OLD GLORY

OLD **G**LORY; 41" x 51"; 5" blocks; made by the author.

Picnics, fireworks, hot summer days—this quilt brings it all together! Pull up a chair in the shade, sip on a long cool drink, and enjoy the lazy days of summer.

> *Summer is the time when one sheds one's tensions with one's clothes, and the right kind of day is jeweled balm for the battered spirit. A few of those days and you can become drunk with the belief that all's right with the world.*
>
> *— Ada Louise Huxtable*

FABRIC REQUIREMENTS

- Red print: 1¼ yd.
- White print: 1 yd.
- Blue print: 1⅓ yd.
- Backing: 2⅔ yd.
- Batting: Twin size

ADDITIONAL REQUIREMENTS

- Freezer paper or fusible web (½ yd.)

65

CUTTING DIRECTIONS

From	Cut	To Yield
Red print	24—1½" × 42" strips	Strip sets
	1—3½" × 42" strip	4—3½" × 3½" squares
White print	16—1½" × 42" strips	Strip sets
Blue print	2—5½" × 42" strips	13—5½" × 5½" squares
	5—3½" × 42" strips	Border
	2¼" bias strips	225" of bias binding

ASSEMBLING THE RAIL FENCE BLOCKS (Make 50)

Step 1: Sew three red 1½" × 42" strips and two white 1½" × 42" strips together to form a strip set. Press the seams toward the red strips, being careful to keep the strip set straight, not curved. At this point the strip set should measure 5½" wide. If not, adjust your seam allowance. Make 8 strip sets.

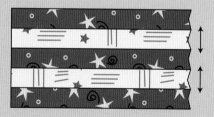

Step 2: Cut the strip sets into 50—5½" × 5½" rail fence blocks.

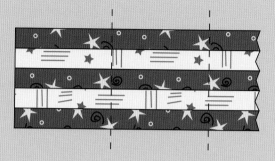

ASSEMBLING THE STAR BLOCKS (Make 13)

Step 1: Trace thirteen stars (see opposite page) onto the dull side of freezer paper or the paper side of fusible web. (See page 17 for more instruction on both appliqué techniques.)

Step 2: Iron the fusible web or the freezer paper to the wrong side of the white print.

Step 3: The stars can be fused or hand- or machine-appliquéd with turned-under edges onto the blue 5½" squares.

100%

Tip

With the traditional appliqué, you can trim
the blue background from behind the star
so it doesn't shadow through.

ASSEMBLING THE QUILT

Step 1: Arrange the star blocks and rail fence blocks as shown in the quilt assembly diagram on opposite page, or create your own arrangement. Sew the blocks together in rows. Press the seams toward the vertical rail fence blocks.

Step 2: Sew the rows together, pinning and matching seam allowances. Press the row seams all one direction.

BORDERS

Step 1: Measure the quilt width through the middle and trim two 3½" x 42" blue border lengths to this measurement.

Step 2: Join the remaining three 3½" x 42" blue border strips. Measure the length of the quilt and cut two side borders to this length. Sew the red 3½" squares to the ends of the side border strips. Press toward the border strips.

Step 3: Sew the shorter borders to the top and bottom of the quilt. Press toward the borders.

Step 4: Sew the remaining borders to the sides of the quilt. Press toward the borders.

FINISHING THE QUILT

Step 1: Piece the backing. Trim the batting and backing 3" larger than the quilt top on all sides. Layer the backing wrong side up, the batting, and then the quilt top right side up. Baste.

Step 2: Quilt as desired. The quilt shown was machine-quilted in the ditch between the blocks. Hand-quilting was done around each star and in the ditch in each rail fence block. The border was hand-stitched in parallel lines 1" apart (like piano keys).

Step 3: Before binding, hand-baste a scant ¼" from the edge of the quilt to hold the layers together and prevent shifting while the binding is being sewn on.

BINDING

Step 1: Bind with 2¼"-wide blue double bias binding strips joined with diagonal seams pressed open. (See page 11-12 for cutting and preparing the binding.) Fold the binding in half and press.

Step 2: Sew the binding on with a ¼" seam, mitering the corners (see page 13 for more instruction on mitering corners).

Step 3: Join the binding ends with the "Perfect Fit" technique shown on page 15.

Step 4: Trim the excess batting and backing, and turn the binding to the back side and stitch down by hand with matching thread.

Sign and date your patriotic wall-hanging!

OLD GLORY quilt assembly

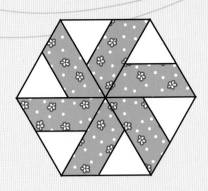

August
HOLLYHOCK GARDEN

HOLLYHOCK GARDEN; 48½" x 56½"; 6" blocks; made by the author.

The Hollyhock Garden quilt was photographed with the Chook House or hen house in the background. No farmyard would be complete without a few chickens in residence, or the girls as Judy calls them. Each of the girls has a name and a personality. While they do have their own Chook House, the girls are free spirits and roam at will.

One simple shape is used in the construction of this quilt—a 60-degree triangle. You'll find it surprisingly easy to piece since there are no set-in seams. The extra triangles you cut from the strip sets can be used to make another quilt of any size (see the Garden Pinwheels pattern on page 78).

FABRIC REQUIREMENTS

- ∞ Vintage white: 2⅔ yd.
- ∞ Variety of prints: 15 fat quarters
- ∞ Green (Aloe) solid: 1½ yd.
- ∞ Backing: 3 yd.
- ∞ Batting: Twin size

SUGGESTED TOOLS

See Tool Tutorials on pages 118–123.

- ∞ Equilateral 60-Degree Triangle

CUTTING DIRECTIONS

From	Cut	Yield
Vintage white	45—2" x 42" strips	90—2" x 21" strips for strip sets
From each print	6—2" x 21" strips	Strip sets
Green solid	10—3½" x 42" strips	116—3½"—60 degree triangles*
	3—2" x 42" strips	Top and bottom borders
	7—1¼" x 42" strips	Binding

* *If not using the Equilateral 60-Degree Triangle, use the template on page 76.*

ASSEMBLING THE BLOCKS (Make 60)

Step 1: Sew the white and print 2" x 21" strips together to make 90 strip sets. Press toward the print strips.

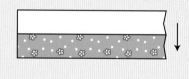

Tip

Finger press the strips before ironing. Keep the strip set straight, not curved.

Step 2: Using the Equilateral 60-Degree Triangle or template on page 76, cut A-triangles and B-triangles. Cut 24 A-triangles from each print. (Six A-triangles are needed for each flower.) Set aside the B-triangles for GARDEN PINWHEELS page 78.

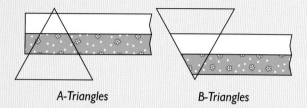

A-Triangles *B-Triangles*

Step 3: Sew together three matching A-triangles, and press exactly as shown. No need to trim off the extended points (*dog-ears*). Instead, use the extended points to align the next unit. Make a second unit exactly the same, and press.

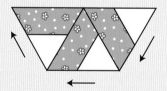

Step 4: Sew the two identical halves together to make a flower, matching up the extended points and the centers. Twist the center seam to open it, and press half the seam one direction, half the other. (See page 10 for this technique.) In the same manner, make a total of 60 flowers, one more than needed.

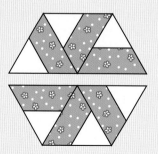

ASSEMBLING THE QUILT

Step 1: Matching extended points, sew the green triangles to the upper left and bottom right corners, turning the hexagon flower units into diamonds. Sew only *one* triangle to the last ten flower units.

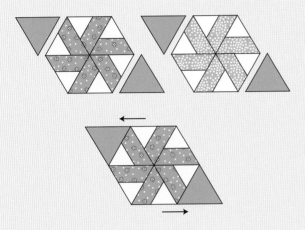

Step 2: Sew the flowers together in rows, pinning and matching the center horizontal seam. Twist the seam in the center to open so the seams go in opposite directions. Sew five rows with seven flowers, using the flower units with only one green triangle at each end as shown.

Step 3: Sew four rows with six flowers, adding an extra green triangle at each end as shown.

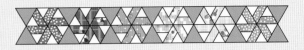

Step 4: Sew the rows together, pinning and matching at each seam intersection. Alternate the rows of seven with the rows of six. Press the seams all one direction.

BORDERS

Step 1: From the 2" x 42" green solid strips, piece border strips longer than necessary for the top and bottom of the quilt. Sew to the quilt, pressing toward the border. Trim off the border ends at the same angle as the flower blocks.

FINISHING THE QUILT

Step 1: Prepare the backing 3" to 4" larger than the quilt top. Trim the batting to approximately the same size as the backing.

Step 2: Layer, with the backing wrong side up, the batting, then the quilt top, right side up. Pin or thread-baste the layers together.

Step 3: Quilt as desired. The quilt shown was machine-stitched in the ditch between all the "petals" of the flowers. Each of the green triangles was hand-stitched ¼" from the seam. A small cable was quilted in the top and bottom borders.

Step 4: Before binding, hand-baste a scant ¼" from the edge of the quilt to hold the layers together and prevent shifting.

BINDING

Step 1: Join the 1¼" binding strips with diagonal seams pressed open. (See page 11-12 for more information on preparing binding.)

Step 2: Sew the binding to the quilt with a ¼" seam, matching the raw edge of the binding to the raw edge of the quilt top.

Step 3: At the inside corners, stitch to the bottom of the "V," stop with the needle down, and pivot at the corner, pulling the quilt and the binding around the needle. Push the pleat that forms in front of the needle *behind* the needle. Lower the presser foot and stitch out of the corner, being careful not to stitch any pleats into the binding, (See page 14 for more instruction on this technique.)

Step 4: At the outside corners, miter as usual. (See page 13 for mitering corners.)

Step 5: Join binding ends with the "Perfect Fit" binding technique shown on page 15.

Step 6: Trim excess batting and backing, turn the binding under ¼", and stitch down by hand on the back side of the quilt with matching thread, covering the stitching line. At the "Vs," a little pleat should form on both the front and the back of the quilt.

Remember to sign and date!

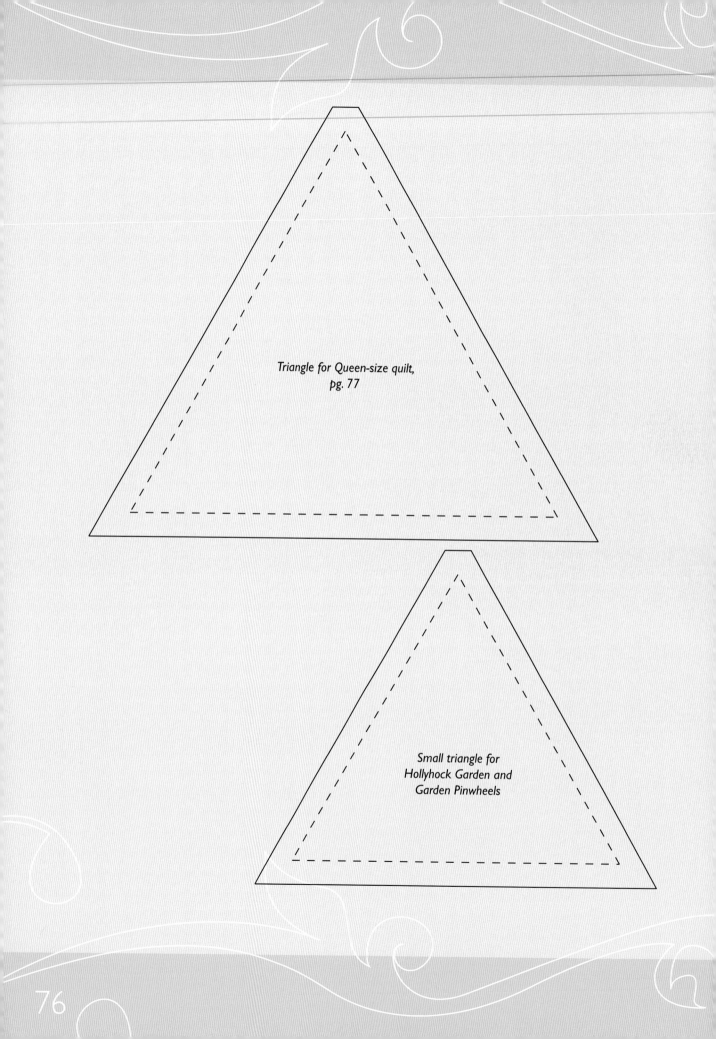

Triangle for Queen-size quilt,
pg. 77

Small triangle for
Hollyhock Garden and
Garden Pinwheels

HOLLYHOCK GARDEN
(Queen-Size)

Finished Size, 96" x 110", 8" blocks. Set 12 x 13 for a total of 150 flower blocks.

Note: With the extra B triangles, you can make a second quilt! (You will only need to purchase another 4¼ yd. of green.)

FABRIC REQUIREMENTS AND SUGGESTED TOOLS

- ∞ Vintage White: 10½ yd.
- ∞ Variety of Prints: 50 fat quarters
- ∞ Green Solid: 4¼ yd.
- ∞ Equilateral 60-Degree Triangle (or the large template on page 76)

96" x 110" CUTTING DIRECTIONS

From the print fabrics, cut six 2½" strips from each fat quarter for strip sets. You can cut three flowers (18 A-triangles) from each fat quarter, or three A-triangles from each strip set.

From the white fabric, cut 150—2½" x 42" strips to make 300—2½" x 21" strips.

From the green fabric for the triangles, cut 25—4½" x 42" strips then cut into 298—4½" triangles (see large template on previous page or use the 4½" size on the Equilateral 60-Degree Triangle). For the borders, cut 6—3½" x 42" strips. For the binding, cut 13—1¼" x 42" strips.

Piece the strip sets and sew according to directions on page 72-73. Arrange in seven rows of twelve flowers and green triangles, alternated with six rows of eleven flowers.

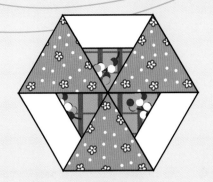

GARDEN PINWHEELS

GARDEN PINWHEELS; 34" x 39"; 6" blocks; made by the author.

A lovely guest house can be found on Lavender Hill Farm—the perfect spot for a retreat in this heavenly place! It doubles as a sales room for the various lavender products produced from the lavender grown on the nearby hillside, so it is redolent of lavender and sunshine. Sit on the front porch and enjoy the scenery with this sweet quilt made with the leftover fabric from the Hollyhock Garden quilt.

Lavender Linen Spray

Add 10-15 drops of essential lavender oil to ½ cup water. Use the spray to scent linens when ironing, or spray pillows, sheets and bedding to help relax and unwind at the end of a tiring day.

FABRIC REQUIREMENTS

- ∾ Green (Aloe) solid: ¾ yd.
- ∾ Print for border: ⅓ yd.
- ∾ Leftover print fat quarters and B-triangles from HOLLYHOCK GARDENS quilt
- ∾ Backing: 1⅛ yd.
- ∾ Batting: 38" x 43"

SUGGESTED TOOLS

See Tool Tutorials on pages 118–123.

- ∾ Equilateral 60-Degree Triangle (or use template on page 76)

CUTTING DIRECTIONS

From	Cut	To Yield
Variety of Prints	3½" × 21" strips	3—matching 60-degree triangles for each of 19 "flowers" *
Green solid	4—3½" × 42" strips	36—3½" 60-degree triangles*
	4—2¼" × 42" strips	Binding
Print for border	3—3" × 42" strips	Border

Or use small template on page 76.

ASSEMBLING THE BLOCKS

Step 1: Sew three matching B-triangles (leftover from the HOLLYHOCK GARDEN quilt) together with three different matching print triangles as shown. Press all the seams to the right.

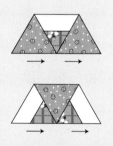

Step 2: Sew the two halves of the flowers together, pinning and matching the center seam intersection. Twist the center to open. (See page 10 for this technique.) Repeat to make a total of 19 flowers.

ASSEMBLING THE QUILT

Step 1: Arrange the flower blocks in two rows of three flowers, two rows of four flowers, and one row of five flowers as shown in the illustration.

Step 2: Following the illustration below as a guide, sew the green triangles on opposite sides of *most* of the flower blocks. The two top rows of the quilt have one green triangle added in a different location. Press the seams toward the green triangles.

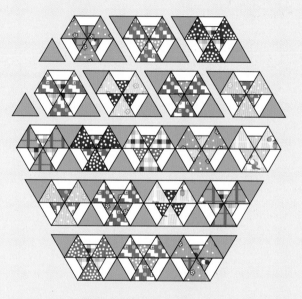

Step 3: Sew the flower blocks together in rows, matching and pinning the centers and ends. Twist the center seam to open (see page 10 for this technique). Press the seams.

Step 4: Sew the rows together. Press the seams all one direction.

BORDERS

Step 1: Measure and trim one 3"-wide print border slightly longer than the length of one side of the quilt. Sew to the quilt, and press toward the border. Trim both ends off at the same angle as the quilt.

Step 2: Measure and trim one 3"-wide border slightly longer than the length of one side plus the border already sewn on. Sew to an adjacent side of the quilt and press toward the border. Trim the edges evenly with the quilt. Continue in this manner around the edge of the quilt.

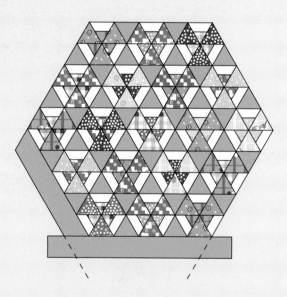

FINISHING THE QUILT

Step 1: Trim batting and backing approximately 4" larger all around than the quilt top. Place the backing right side down, the batting, then the quilt top right side up. Baste.

Step 2: Quilt as desired. The quilt shown was machine-stitched in the ditch on all the diagonal lines. Hand-quilting was done ¼" inside each of the green triangles and around the small pinwheel in the flower blocks. A pretty design was hand-quilted in the border.

Step 3: Before binding, hand-baste a scant ¼" from the edge of the quilt to hold all the layers together.

BINDING

Step 1: Prepare the green solid binding by sewing the 2¼"-wide strips together with diagonal seams pressed open. Fold the binding in half, wrong sides together and press.

Step 2: Sew the binding to the quilt with a ¼" seam, mitering the corners as shown on page 13.

Step 3: Join the binding ends with the "Perfect Fit" binding technique described on page 15.

Step 2: Trim the excess batting and backing, then turn the binding over the raw edge and stitch down by hand with matching thread.

Sign and date!

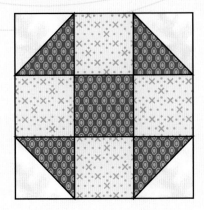

September
BLUEBERRIES AND CREAM TABLE RUNNER

BLUEBERRIES AND CREAM; 18" x 42"; 4½" blocks; made by the author.

September is a time of gathering and harvests, summer endings, and school beginnings; a wonderful time of the year. Celebrate this season with a blue and cream table runner to complement the delicious foods you prepare from the fruits of your garden.

Lavender is a culinary friend. Toss one teaspoon or more into your favorite shortbread or sugar cookie recipe. This also makes a delicious addition to a chocolate desert, cakes, jellies, vinegars and more!

FABRIC REQUIREMENTS

- Dark yellow print: ⅜ yd.
- Light yellow print: 1 fat quarter
- Dark blue print: 1 yd.
- Backing: 1¼ yd.
- Batting: 22" x 46" (cotton batting recommended)

SUGGESTED TOOLS

See Tool Tutorials on pages 118–123.

- Easy Angle
- Easy Scallop

CUTTING AND ASSEMBLING CHURN DASH BLOCKS
(Make 10)

From	Cut	To Yield
Dark blue	2—2" x 42" strips	40—Easy Angle Triangles
		1—2" x 21" strip
Light yellow	3—2" x 21" strips	40—Easy Angle Triangles
Dark yellow	1—2" x 42" strip	2—2" x 21" strips
	1—2" x 42" strip	20—2" x 2" squares

If not using Easy Angle, cut 3—2⅜" x 21" strips from light yellow and dark blue. Cut into 20 squares of each color; cut once on the diagonal.

Step 1: Sew together two 2" x 21" dark yellow strips with one 2" x 21" dark blue strip to make a strip set. Press toward the yellow strips. Cut into ten 2" units.

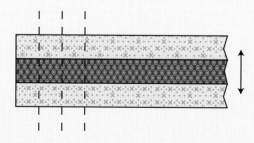

Step 2: Layer a light yellow and a dark blue triangle right sides together. Sew together on the diagonal edge. Press toward the dark blue triangle. Repeat to make 40 triangle squares.

Step 3: Sew a dark yellow square between two of the triangle squares from step 2. Make 20 units. Press toward the dark yellow squares.

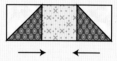

Step 4: Sew the step 1 units between the step 3 units to make a total of ten churn dash blocks. Press the seams toward the block center. At this point the blocks should measure 5".

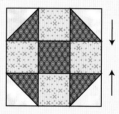

CUTTING AND ASSEMBLING ALTERNATE BLOCKS (Make 7)

From	Cut	To Yield
Dark yellow	2—2" × 42" strips	4—2" × 21" strips
Light yellow	4—2" × 21" strips	Strip sets
Dark blue	1—2" × 42" strip	2—2" × 21" strips

Step 1: Sew together two strip sets of dark yellow and light yellow. Press toward the dark yellow strips. Cut into fourteen 2" units.

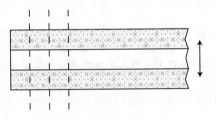

Step 2: Sew together one strip set of light yellow and dark blue. Press toward the dark blue strip. Cut into seven 2" units.

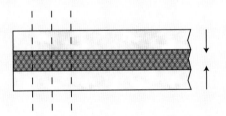

Step 3: Sew together the step 1 and step 2 units to make seven alternate blocks. Press toward the dark yellow squares. At this point the blocks should measure 5".

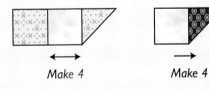

CUTTING AND ASSEMBLING SETTING TRIANGLES

From	Cut	To Yield
Dark yellow	1—3¾" × 3¾" square	Cut once on the diagonal for the 2 end pieces
	2—3½" × 3½" squares	Cut twice on the diagonal for 8 triangles
		4—2" × 2" squares
Light yellow	1—2" × 21" strip	8—2" × 2" squares
Dark blue	1—3¼" × 3¼" square	Cut twice on the diagonal for 4 triangles
	3—2½" × 42" strips	Borders

Step 1: Sew the squares and triangles together in rows and press as directed.

Make 4   *Make 4*

Step 2: Sew the rows together, adding the last dark yellow triangles. Make four pieced setting triangles and press as shown.

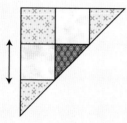

ASSEMBLING THE TABLE RUNNER

Step 1: Sew together the churn dash block, two pieced setting triangles, and one end triangle as shown. Press. Make 2.

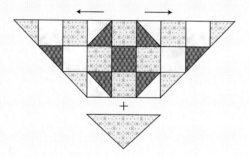

Step 2: Sew the remaining blocks together in rows, following the diagram on page 89. Press the seams toward the alternate blocks.

Step 3: Sew the rows together, matching and pinning seam intersections. Add the sections from step 1 to the ends. Press the seams all one direction.

BORDERS

Step 1: Sew one blue border strip to one short end of the table runner. Press toward the border and trim off evenly with the sides of the table runner. Repeat at the opposite end.

Step 2: Sew a blue border strip to the other short end of the table runner. Press and trim as before. Repeat for the opposite end of the runner.

Step 3: Sew blue border strips to the long sides of the table runner, pressing toward the borders and trimming even.

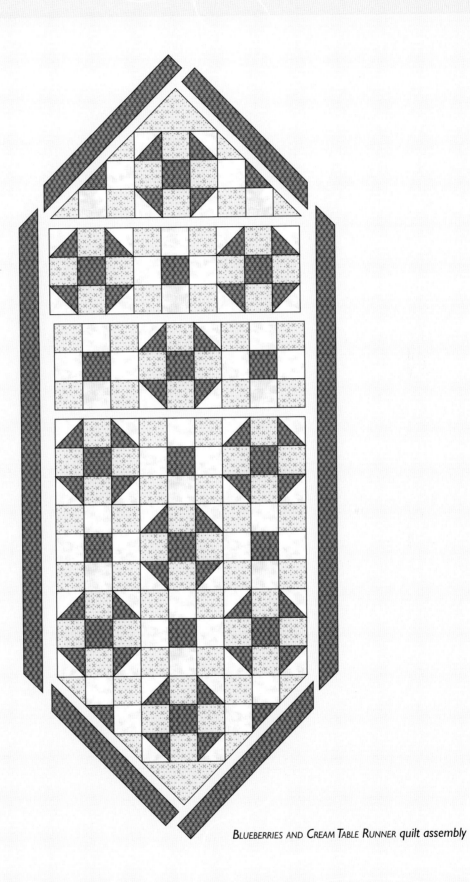

BLUEBERRIES AND CREAM TABLE RUNNER *quilt assembly*

FINISHING THE TABLE RUNNER

Step 1: Before quilting, mark the edges of the table runner with Easy Scallop set at 4". Mark any quilting lines. (See page 122 for more instruction on marking scalloped edges.)

Step 2: Trim the backing and batting about 2" larger than the quilt top on all sides. Layer with the backing wrong side up, the batting and then the quilt top right side up. Baste.

Step 3: Quilt as desired. The quilt shown was machine-meandered with yellow thread on the yellow areas, and blue thread in the blue border.

Step 4: Hand-baste along the marked outer edge to hold the layers together.

BINDING

Step 1: From the remaining dark blue fabric, cut 1¼" *bias* binding strips to measure about 140". Join with diagonal seams pressed open. See pages 11-12 for more information on preparing bias binding.

Step 2: Sew to the quilt with a ¼" seam, pivoting at the "Vs." See pages 13-14 for instruction on binding a scalloped edge.

Step 3: Join the binding ends with the "Perfect Fit" technique (see page 15).

Step 4: Trim the excess batting and backing to an even ¼". Turn the binding to the back side and stitch down by hand with matching thread.

Sign and enjoy!

October
PUMPKIN PATCH

Pᴜᴍᴘᴋɪɴ Pᴀᴛᴄʜ; 44" x 44"; 12" blocks; pieced, appliquéd, and quilted by the author.

Cool crisp days, the rustle of fallen leaves underfoot, the smell of pumpkin pie baking in the oven—fall is here! This wall quilt, shown draped on a rustic wagon, is the perfect quilt to bring the colors of fall into your home. The appliquéd pumpkin blocks are enhanced with embroidery and are a nice complement to the colorful pieced sashings. The prairie-point edge finish adds a nice three-dimensional touch to the quilt, and is quite easy to do.

Pumpkin Spice Mocha

Makes one 6-8 oz. cup. *Adjust the spice to your taste.

²⁄₃ cup coffee
¹⁄₃ cup milk
1 ½ tsp. unsweetened cocoa powder
¼-½ tsp. pumpkin pie spice*

Combine the hot coffee, with warm milk and add cocoa powder, sugar and pumpkin pie spice. Great to take the chill off a cold October evening.

FABRIC REQUIREMENTS

- Light tan background: ⅝ yd.
- Medium tan background for setting triangles: 1 yd.
- Brown print for border and binding: 1 yd.
- Orange print for pumpkins: fat quarter
- Dark prints in fall colors: totaling approximately 1 ½ yd.
- Light prints in fall colors: totaling ¾ yd.
- Backing: 2¾ yd.
- Batting: 50" x 50"

ADDITIONAL SUPPLIES

- Embroidery floss in dark green and dark orange
- Fusible web for fusible appliqué or freezer paper for turned-under appliqué
- Glue Baste-It (optional)

SUGGESTED TOOLS

See Tool Tutorials on pages 118–123.

- Flip-n-Set
- Easy Angle

CUTTING DIRECTIONS

From	Cut	To Yield
Light tan background	2—9" × 42" strips	5—9" × 9" squares
Medium tan background	2—6½" × 42" strips*	4—Flip-n-Set triangles*
	1—7" × 42" strip	2—7" squares cut once on the diagonal for corners
	5—2½" × 42" strips	Outer border
Variety of light prints	2½" strips**	136—Easy Angle triangles**
		12—2½" × 2½" squares
Variety of dark prints	2½" strips**	136—Easy Angle triangles**
		12—2½" × 2½" squares
	56—4" × 4" squares	Prairie point edge
Brown print	4—4" × 42" strips	Inner border
	1— 2½" × 42" strip	4—2½" × 2½" squares for corners
	2¼" bias strips	Binding

*If not using Flip-n-Set, cut one 13" square; cut twice on the diagonal.

**If not using Easy Angle, cut 2⅞" squares; cut once on the diagonal.

ASSEMBLING THE PUMPKIN BLOCKS (Make 5)

Step 1: Using the reversed templates (page 97), trace five pumpkins, five stems, and ten leaves on either freezer paper or fusible webbing. Fuse or prepare the pieces for appliqué (see page 17 for more instruction on appliqué techniques).

Step 2: Fuse, pin, or glue baste the appliqué shapes in place *on the diagonal* of the background squares. Appliqué by hand or machine.

Step 3: Add the vine and details to the pumpkin and leaves with two strands of embroidery floss and an outline stitch. (Use the illustration on page 101 to trace vines).

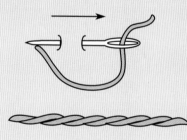

Outline stitch

Note: The vine and details can be traced using a blue wash-out pen, chalk, or light pencil lines. Do not iron over the blue marks because heat will set them as permanent.

Step 4: To remove the blue wash-out pen marks soak the blocks in cold water. To remove any starch and glue, soak in warm water. Lay flat to dry, then press right side down on a fluffy towel. *Trim the blocks to an even 8½" x 8½".*

PIECED SASHING FOR PUMPKIN BLOCKS

Step 1: Matching a light triangle to a dark triangle, sew together 128 triangle squares. *Note there will be eight light and eight dark triangles left over. Press toward the darker triangle.*

Step 2: Arrange sixteen triangle squares, two light squares, and two dark squares around four of the pumpkin blocks as shown. Join the triangle squares and squares in rows and sew to all four sides of each of four pumpkin blocks. Press the seams as shown. Make 4.

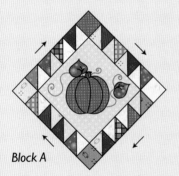

Block A

Step 3: Arrange sixteen triangle squares, two light squares, and two dark squares around the remaining pumpkin block as shown. Join the triangle squares in rows and sew to all sides of the block. Press the seams as shown. Make 1.

Block B

ASSEMBLING SETTING AND CORNER TRIANGLE UNITS

Step 1: Arrange eight triangle squares, one light square, and two dark triangles around a setting triangle. Press as shown. Make 2 setting triangles A.

Note: The setting triangles are larger than needed, so put any excess fabric on the outer edge.

Step 2: Arrange eight triangle squares, one dark square, and two light triangles around the remaining two setting triangles. Press as shown. Make 2 setting triangles B.

Step 3: Arrange four triangle squares, a light triangle, and a dark triangle on the long edge of a smaller corner triangle. Press one to the right and one to the left. Make 2 corner triangles A.

Note: Center the pieced strip on the bias edge and sew with the triangles on top to prevent stretching.

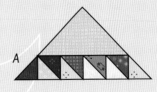

Step 4: Arrange four triangle squares, a light triangle, and a dark triangle on the long edges of the remaining two smaller corner triangles as before. Sew, then press one to the right and one to the left. Make 2 corner triangles B.

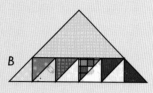

ASSEMBLING THE QUILT

Step 1: Starting in left upper corner, sew one corner triangle A, one pumpkin block A, one setting triangle A, and one setting triangle B as shown. Make two; one is the bottom-right unit. Press the seams open.

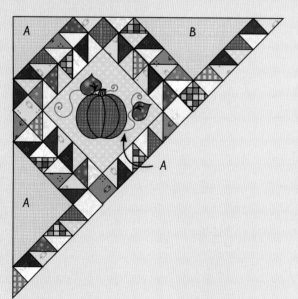

Step 2: Sew the remaining two pumpkin blocks A and the pumpkin block B together with two corner triangle Bs. Press the seams open.

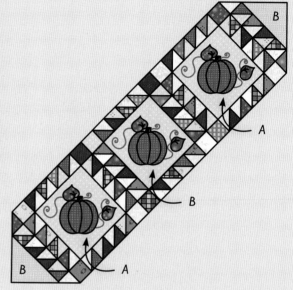

Step 3: Join the three quilt segments together, pinning and matching seam intersections. Press the seams open. Trim the edges straight, leaving at least a ¼" seam allowance around the edge.

*Reversed for
tracing templates*

BORDERS

Step 1: Measure and trim two 4" brown print borders to the width of the quilt. Sew to the quilt. Press toward the borders just added. (See page 11 for more instruction on adding borders.)

Step 2: Repeat this procedure for the sides of the quilt.

Step 3: Measure and trim four medium tan 2½" borders the width and length of the quilt. Sew borders to the top and bottom of the quilt. Sew brown 2½" squares to the ends of the two remaining borders. Sew the borders with cornerstones to the sides of the quilt. Press toward the borders.

PRAIRIE POINT EDGING

Step 1: Using the 56 dark 4" x 4" squares, press in half once on the diagonal. Press again on the diagonal to make prairie points. Make 56.

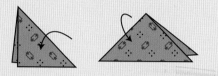

Step 2: Position the prairie points along the edge of the quilt top, points facing in, just touching the cornerstones. The prairie points tuck inside one another approximately ¼" and they are adjustable to fit the border. Place fourteen on each side of the quilt. Sew on with a scant ¼" seam.

ADDING EMBROIDERY

Trace the leaf-and-vine design on page 100 onto the large and small setting triangles with chalk, light pencil lines or blue wash-out pen. (Remove the blue marks by soaking in cold water.) Embroider with two strands of green floss.

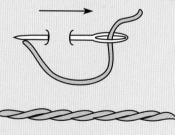

Outline stitch

PUMPKIN PATCH *quilt assembly*

FINISHING THE QUILT

Step 1: Piece the backing, then trim 3" to 4" larger than the quilt top. Trim the batting to the same size.

Step 2: Layer the backing wrong side up, the batting, and then the quilt top right side up. Baste.

Step 3: Quilt as desired. The quilt shown was hand-quilted around the pumpkin motifs, and a grid was quilted in the background of the pumpkin blocks as well as the setting and corner triangles. The triangle squares were quilted in the ditch. A leaf-and-vine design was quilted in the brown border, and a machine meander was quilted in the last border. (You can quilt underneath the prairie points if so desired; just lift them out of the way while quilting.)

Step 4: Baste a scant ¼" from the edge of the quilt to hold the layers together while binding.

BINDING

Step 1: Join the 2¼" brown print bias binding strips with diagonal seams pressed open. Fold in half lengthwise, wrong sides together, and press. Sew the binding to the quilt with a ¼" seam, mitering the corners. (See page 11-13 for more instruction on binding.)

Step 2: Join the binding ends with the "Perfect Fit" technique. See page 15 for more instruction.

Step 3: Trim excess batting and backing, turn to the back side and stitch down by hand with matching thread.

Sign and date your PUMPKIN PATCH quilt!

Embroidery design for setting triangles and corner triangles

Use for embroidery
placement

November
AUTUMN SPLENDOR

AUTUMN SPLENDOR; 24" × 42"; 8" blocks; pieced, appliquéd, and quilted by the author.

By late summer, the flowers are beginning to fade and the leaves start to turn color. The farm, nestled in the hills and valleys of Oregon, now wears the brilliant shades of autumn—the bright reds, oranges, and yellows. In this quilt the fall leaf colors sparkle as jewel tones against a midnight black background. Celebrate the beautiful colors of the autumn season!

> *There is a harmony in autumn, and a luster in its sky, which through the summer is not heard or seen, as if it could not be, as if it had not been!*
>
> — *Percy Bysshe Shelley*

FABRIC REQUIREMENTS

- Black solid: 1¼ yd.
- Variety of prints: fat quarters or fat eighths of green, gold, red, and brown
- Backing: 1⅓ yd.
- Batting: 28" × 46"

ADDITIONAL SUPPLIES

- Freezer paper or fusible web
- Glue Baste-It (optional)
- Black embroidery floss

SUGGESTED TOOLS

See Tool Tutorials on pages 118–123.

- Easy Angle
- Companion Angle

CUTTING DIRECTIONS

From	Cut	To Yield
Black solid	1—9" x 42" strip	2—9" x 9" squares
	10—2½" x 42" strips	50—Companion Angle triangles*
		8—2½" x 4½" rectangles
		2—2½" x 6½" rectangles
		12—2½" x 2½" squares
		2—2½" x 34½" sashing strips
		3—2½" x 16½" sashing strips
	4—2¼" x 42" strips	150" double binding
Variety of prints	13—2½" x 21" strips	100—Easy Angle triangles**
		32—2½" x 2½" squares

*If not using Companion Angle, cut 13—5¼" squares; cut twice on the diagonal.

**If not using Easy Angle, cut 50—2⅞" squares; cut once diagonally.

APPLIQUÉING THE BLOCKS (Make 2)

Step 1: Using the reversed pattern on page 109, trace the shapes on either freezer paper or fusible web. See page 17 for more instruction on freezer paper or fusible web appliqué.

Step 2: Fuse or appliqué the shapes onto the 9" black squares. Refer to the quilt picture on page 102 for placement of the leaves and acorns. Add embroidered veins on the leaves with two strands of black embroidery floss. Make two blocks. When the appliqué is finished (and the blocks are washed and pressed) *trim the blocks to 8½" x 8½"*.

ASSEMBLING THE BLOCKS

Step 1: Sew a small colored triangle to the right side of a larger black triangle. Press toward the colored triangle. Repeat to make 50 units.

Step 2: Sew a different colored triangle to the left side of the step 1 unit. Press toward the colored triangle. Make 50 flying geese units. At this point the units should measure 2½" x 4½".

Step 3: Sew three flying geese units (from step 2) together with two colored squares to make the unit shown below. Press as indicated. Make 8 units. At this point the units should measure 4½" x 8½".

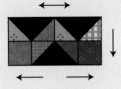

Step 4: Sew a unit from step 3 to the top of the appliquéd block and another one to the bottom of the block. Press the seams toward the appliquéd block. Repeat for the second appliquéd block.

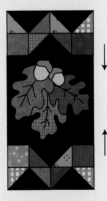

Step 5: Sew a colored square to a black square. Repeat to make 8 of these units. Press toward the colored square.

Step 6: Sew a 2½" x 4½" black rectangle to the bottom of the step 5 units. Press toward the rectangle. Make 8 of these units. At this point the units should measure 4½" x 4½".

Step 7: Sew the step 6 units to both ends of the remaining step 3 units. Press toward the step 6 units. Make 4.

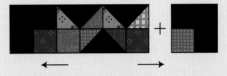

Step 8: Sew the units from step 7 to the sides of the blocks. Press toward the appliqué blocks. Make 2 blocks. At this point the blocks should measure 16½" x 16½".

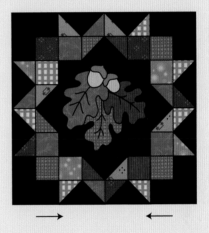

Step 9: Sew the 2½" x 16½" black sashing strips between the two blocks and to the top and bottom of the quilt. Press toward the sashing.

Step 10: Sew four colored squares to the ends of the 2½" x 34½" sashing strips. Press toward the sashing. Sew to the sides of the quilt. Press toward the sashing.

BORDERS

Step 1: Sew together five flying geese units for the top and bottom borders. Press the seams open. Sew to the top and bottom of the quilt. Press toward the black sashing strips.

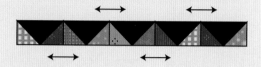

Step 2: Place a colored square on the corner of a 2½" × 6½" black rectangle. Mark a diagonal line on the square and sew on the line. Trim the seam allowance to ¼", and press toward the colored triangle. Repeat on the opposite corner. Make 2 units.

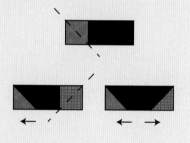

Step 3: Sew together four flying geese units. Press the seams open. Make 4 units.

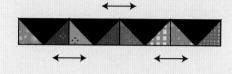

Step 4: Sew a step 2 unit between two step 3 units. Press the seams open. Sew a black square to both ends of the borders. Make 2.

Step 5: Sew the side borders to the quilt, pressing the seams toward the black sashing strips.

> ### Tip
>
> *If the pieced borders don't quite fit the quilt top, the black sashing can be trimmed evenly, or wider sashing can be added.*

AUTUMN SPLENDOR quilt assembly

FINISHING THE QUILT

Step 1: Trim the backing 2" larger than the quilt top on all sides. Trim the batting to the same size. Layer the backing wrong side up, the batting, and then the quilt top right side up, and baste.

Step 2: Quilt as desired. The quilt shown was machine-stippled in the black background with black thread. Black thread was stitched by hand in the colored triangles and in the appliqué blocks.

Step 3: Before binding, hand-baste a scant ¼" from the edge of the quilt to hold the layers together.

BINDING

Step 1: Join the black 2¼" × 42" binding strips with diagonal seams pressed open. Fold the binding in half, wrong sides together, and press to make a double binding. (See page 11 for more instructions on preparing binding.)

Step 2: Sew to the quilt with a ¼" seam, mitering the corners. (See page 13 for more instruction on mitering corners.)

Step 3: Join the binding ends with the "Perfect Fit" technique described on page 15.

Step 4: Trim the excess batting and backing, and stitch down the back side by hand with matching thread.

Sign and date!

*Reversed for
tracing templates*

December
WINTER COZY

Winter Cozy; 93" x 104"; 11" blocks; made by the author.

This is the best month of the year! For many of us the first snowfall comes in December, and the landscape is magically transformed to one of white sparkling beauty. Then it's time to sit by the fire sipping hot chocolate, keeping the toes toasty in this warm, cuddly WINTER COZY quilt. Use a lightweight wool batt for extra softness and warmth during the winter months.

Tip

This pineapple pattern may look difficult, but in reality is simple to do, and is a great project for using up scraps! There is quite a bit of cutting and sewing involved, so I recommend breaking up the time spent at each task. Cut for twenty minutes or so, then sew for an equal amount of time. Changing tasks frequently is better for your body. I also suggest completing several blocks at a time instead of doing the same step 72 times! You'll have more of a feeling of accomplishment if you finish a few blocks in one sewing session.

FABRIC REQUIREMENTS

- Assortment of light tan, cream, and white prints: 6 yd. total or 25 fat quarters
- Assortment of red prints: 10 yd. total or 40 fat quarters
- Red print for block centers, border, and binding: 2⅝ yd.
- Batting: Queen size
- Backing: 8¼ yd.

Tip

You can choose a different color scheme, but separate your lights and darks. Your light fabrics can range from white to almost a dark tan, and your dark fabrics can also be a wide range of hues and intensities.

Fan out the fabrics you have chosen so you see equal amounts of each. Step back and squint. How do they look? Remove any that don't look quite right, or add more of whatever seems lacking. Play with the fabrics until you like the mix of colors.

CUTTING DIRECTIONS FOR PINEAPPLE BLOCKS

From	Cut	To Yield
From a variety of light prints	144—2½" × 21" strips	1,152— 2½" × 2½" squares
	29—2" × 21" strips	288—2" × 2" squares
From a variety of red prints	432—1½" × 21" strips	144—1½ × 11½" rectangles
		288—1½ × 9½" rectangles
		288—1½ × 7½" rectangles
		288—1½ × 5½" rectangles
		144—1½ × 3½" rectangles
Red print for block centers	7—3½" × 42" strips	72—3½" × 3½" squares
	10—3" × 42" strips	Border
	2¼" bias strips	Enough for 425" of bias binding

Tip

Organize the fabric pieces for this project using inexpensive paper plates. Put all the pieces you need for one block on a plate; place another plate on top and fill it with the pieces for the next block, and so on. Then, when you have a few minutes to sew, you can sit down and complete one or more blocks quickly without having to search out the pieces you need. This method works particularly well with scrap quilts when you wish to distribute your colors evenly.

ASSEMBLING THE BLOCK CENTERS

Step 1: Mark a diagonal line on the wrong side of all the 2" and 2½" assorted light squares.

Note: Using a cutting mat under the squares while marking prevents them from stretching.

Step 2: Align a 2" × 2" light square on the corner of a 3½" × 3½" red square. Sew on the diagonal line. Trim the seam allowance to ¼", and press the seam allowance toward the red square. Repeat on the opposite corner. Make 72.

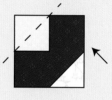

Step 3: In the same manner, sew light 2" × 2" squares to the remaining two corners of the red squares. Trim and press the seam allowances toward the light triangles. Make 72 block centers. At this point the units should measure 3½" × 3½".

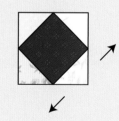

ASSEMBLING THE BLOCKS

Step 1: Sew 1½" x 3½" red rectangles to opposite sides of the block centers. Press the seam allowances away from the center. Make 72.

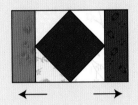

Step 2: Sew 1½" x 5½" red rectangles to the remaining two sides of the block. Press the seam allowances away from the centers. Make 72. At this point the blocks should measure 5½" x 5½".

Note: If you find that the 5½" rectangles are too long or too short, adjust your seam allowances accordingly.

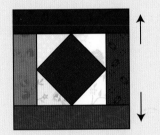

Step 3: Position four marked 2½" x 2½" light squares on the corners of the blocks as shown. Sew on the line, trim the seam allowances to ¼", and press toward the triangles. The blocks should still measure 5½" x 5½". Repeat for all 72 blocks.

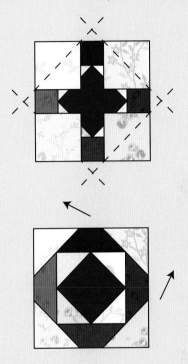

Step 4: Continue to add rectangles and squares around the block in the same manner until the block is complete. Press two opposite triangles on the last round toward the inside of the block, and the other two opposite triangles toward the outside of the block. This will allow the seams to interlock when sewing the blocks together. At this point the blocks should measure 11½" x 11½". Make 72 blocks.

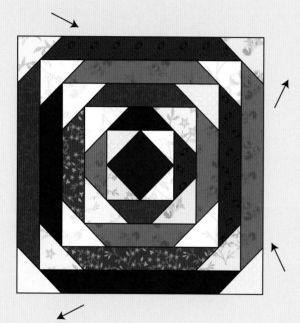

ASSEMBLE THE QUILT TOP

Step 1: Arrange the blocks in nine rows of eight blocks. Sew the blocks together in horizontal rows, using to the WINTER COZY quilt assembly diagram on opposite page as reference. Press all of the seam allowances in each row in one direction, alternating the direction with each row.

Step 2: Join the rows, pinning and matching the seam intersections. Press the seam allowances all in one direction.

BORDERS

Step 1: Using the 3"-wide red border strips, piece, press, and trim two border strips the width of the quilt. Sew to the top and bottom of the quilt. Press the seam allowances toward the borders.

Step 2: Piece, press and trim two borders the exact length of the quilt. Sew these to the sides of the quilt and press the seam allowances toward the borders.

WINTER COZY quilt assembly

FINISHING THE QUILT

Step 1: Piece the backing, then trim it 3" larger than the quilt top on all sides. Trim the batting to the same size. Layer the backing wrong side up, then the batting, and then the quilt top right side up. Baste.

Step 2: Quilt as desired. The quilt shown was hand-quilted ¼" from the outer edge of each red trapezoid and the inner edge of each triangle, and also inside of each center square. A cable motif was stitched in the border.

Step 3: Before binding, hand-baste a scant ¼" from the edge of the quilt to prevent the layers from shifting when the binding is sewn on.

BINDING

Step 1: Join the 2¼" bias strips with diagonal seams pressed open. (See page 11-12 for more instruction on cutting and preparing bias binding.) Fold and press the binding in half, wrong sides together, to make double bias binding. Make at least 425" of binding.

Step 2: Sew the binding to the quilt with a ¼" seam, mitering the corners. (See page 13 for more instruction on mitering corners.)

Step 3: Join the binding ends with the "Perfect Fit" technique found on page 15.

Step 4: Trim the excess batting and backing, turn to the wrong side and stitch the binding down by hand with matching thread.

Sign and date!

MEASUREMENTS FOR ALTERNATE QUILT SIZES

	Wall	Twin	Full
Finished size	49" x 49"	60" x 82"	82" x 93"
Setting of blocks	4 x 4	5 x 7	7 x 8
Number of blocks	16	35	56

FABRIC REQUIREMENTS FOR ALTERNATE SIZES

Fabric	Wall	Twin	Full
Assorted light fat quarters	6	12	18
Assorted red fat quarters	9	20	31
Red print for block centers, border, and binding	1¼ yd.	1¾ yd.	2⅜ yd.
Batting	55" x 55"	Twin	Full/Queen
Backing	3¼ yd.	5 yd.	7¼ yd.

Tool Tutorials

TRI-RECS TOOLS

To cut Tri triangles, lay the tool on the strip of fabric with the top flat edge at the top of the strip, and a line on the tool aligned with the bottom of the strip. Cut on both sides of the triangle. The patterns will tell you what size strip to cut—always ½" larger than the finished size.

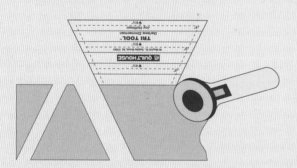

For the second cut, rotate the tool so that it's top edge points down. Align as before, and cut.

To cut Recs triangles, cut the same size strip as for the large triangles. Leave the strip folded and you will automatically cut pairs of Recs triangles. Align the tool with the flat top edge at the top of the strip, and a line on the tool aligned with the bottom of the strip. Cut on the angled edge, then swing around and nip off the *magic angle* at the top.

This needs to be cut accurately; it is your alignment guide when sewing the pieces together.

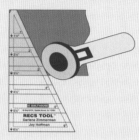

For the second cut, rotate the tool so that it's top edge points down. Align as before and cut, then swing back and trim off the *magic angle*.

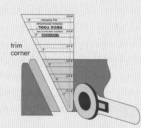

Together the tools cut the shapes for making a triangle within a square. .

Fit the Recs triangle into the corner of the large triangle. Note how the *magic angle* will fit right into the corner as shown. Yes, the pieces look odd at this point, but they will be right when sewn!

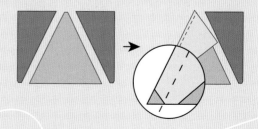

TRIANGLE TABLES FOR TRI-RECS

Use these triangle tables to determine the number of Tri or Recs triangles you can cut from a 42" strip of fabric.

TRI TOOL

Finished Size	Strip Width	Number of Triangles
1"	1½"	38
1½"	2"	31
2"	2½"	25
2½"	3"	21
3"	3½"	19
3½"	4"	17
4"	4½"	15
4½"	5"	13
5"	5½"	12
5½"	6"	11
6"	6½"	10

RECS TOOL

Finished Size	Strip Width	Number of Triangles
1"	1½"	52
1½"	2"	44
2"	2½"	40
2½"	3"	34
3"	3½"	32
3½"	4"	28
4"	4½"	24
4½"	5"	24
5"	5½"	22
5½"	6"	22
6"	6½"	20

EASY ANGLE

This tool comes in two sizes, 4½" and 6½". You may use either one for the projects in this book. Easy Angle allows you to cut triangles from the same size strip as for squares. You only need to add a ½" seam allowance when using Easy Angle, instead of the ⅞" added when not using the tool.

To use the tool most efficiently, layer the fabric strips you are cutting for your triangles right sides together, then cut with Easy Angle. Now they are ready to be chain-sewn.

Before making the first cut, trim off the selvages. Then align the top flat edge of the tool at the top of the strip, matching a line on the tool with the bottom edge of the strip. Cut on the diagonal edge.

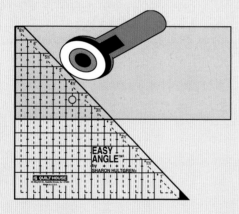

To make the second cut, rotate the tool so the flat edge is aligned at the bottom of the strip, and

a line on the tool is aligned with the top of the strip. Cut again.

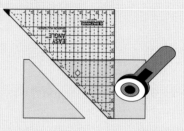

Continue in this manner down the strip. Chain-sew the triangles on the longest edge. Press toward the darkest fabric and trim the *dog-ears*.

Note: If you choose not to use Easy Angle in the projects, you will need to add ⅞" to the finished sizes of the triangle squares. For example, instead of cutting a 2½" strip to yield 2" triangle squares, cut a 2⅞" strip instead. Cut into squares, and cut the squares once on the diagonal.

TRIANGLE TABLES FOR EASY ANGLE

Finished Size of Triangle	From	Number from Strip
½" triangles	1" strip	50
1" triangles	1½" strip	38
1½" triangles	2" strip	30
2" triangles	2½" strip	26
2½" triangles	3" strip	22
3" triangles	3½" strip	20
3½" triangles	4" strip	18
4" triangles	4½" strip	16
4½" triangles	5" strip	14
5" triangles	5½" strip	12
5½" triangles	6" strip	12
6" triangles	6½" strip	12

COMPANION ANGLE

Companion Angle allows you to cut quarter-square triangles—or triangles with the longest edge, on the straight-of-grain. A common use for this type of triangle is the goose in flying geese.

To cut with Companion Angle, align the top flat point of the tool with the top edge of the strip. A line on the tool should align with the bottom of the strip. Cut on both sides of the tool.

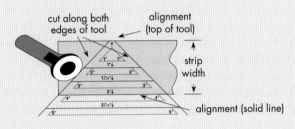

For the next cut, rotate the tool so the point of the tool is at the bottom of the strip, and a line on the tool is aligned with the top of the strip. Cut again. Continue in this manner down the strip of fabric.

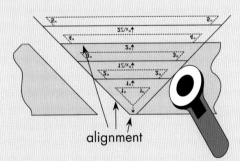

Note: If not using the Companion Angle, you will need to add 1¼" to the finished size of the base of the triangle you are cutting. Cut a square that size, then cut it twice on the diagonal to yield 4 triangles. For example, the goose you are cutting will finish to 3" across the base. Add 1¼" + 3" = 4¼". Cut a 4¼" square, then cut twice to yield 4 triangles.

TRIANGLE TABLES FOR COMPANION ANGLE™

Finished Base of Triangle	From	Number from Strip
1" triangles	1" strip	34
2" triangles	1½" strip	23
3" triangles	2" strip	17
4" triangles	2½" strip	13
5" triangles	3" strip	12
6" triangles	3½" strip	9
7" triangles	4" strip	8
8" triangles	4½" strip	7
9" triangles	5" strip	7
10" triangles	5½" strip	5

EASY SCALLOP

MEASURING

Measure the length of the border. Choose the desired number of scallops. Divide the border length by that number to yield the scallop size. Round the answer to the nearest quarter inch. Set the Easy Scallop tool at that size. For example: 72" border divided by 7 scallops = 10.285". Round to 10¼". Set the tool at 10¼".

MARKING

To mark a rounded corner, begin at the very corner of the quilt and mark a full scallop. Mark from both ends toward the center and adjust the center scallop as needed. When you mark the adjacent edge with a full scallop, the corner will automatically be rounded.

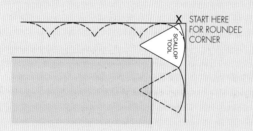

To mark a pointed corner or *ears*, begin at one corner with a half scallop. Again, mark from both ends to the center, adjusting the center scallop as needed. As you mark the adjacent side with a half scallop, the ear will be formed.

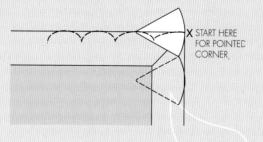

FLIP-N-SET

Step 1: With the tool open, find the *finished size* of the blocks to be set on point and cut strips to the width indicated on the tool.

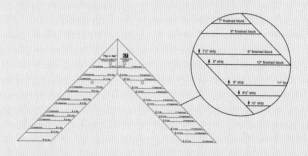

Step 2: Lay the tool on the *opened* strip with the point aligned at the top of the strip. Match the measurement line along the bottom of the strip. Cut on both outside edges of the tool for the first cut.

Note: Flip-n-Set cuts generously sized triangles to allow for trimming.

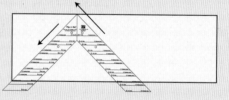

Step 3: Rotate the tool and align the point with the bottom of the strip and the edge of the tool with the edge of the fabric. Make the second cut.

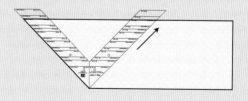

Step 4: Repeat, rotating the tool and cutting to the end of the strip.

Note: For corner triangles, cut two squares the size of the finished blocks. Cut each on the diagonal.

FOR BLOCKS WITH SASHING

Add the *finished width* of one sashing to the *finished size* of the block to determine the size strip to cut for setting triangles. For example, a 12" block plus a 2" sashing makes a 14" block.

EQUILATERAL 60-DEGREE TRIANGLE

Step 1: Cut fabric strips according to the tool. For example, for a 3" finished triangle, cut 3½" strips. Position the triangle at the selvedge end of the strip with the chosen triangle height level with bottom of fabric strip. *The black tip of the triangle should be above the fabric strip.*

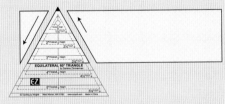

Step 2: Trim and discard the corner on the left side of fabric strip. Cut along the right edge of tool for the first triangle. Rotate the tool, align, and cut again.

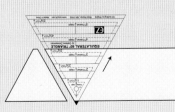

Step 3: Continue in the same manner to the end of the strip.

45-DEGREE DIAMOND

Step 1: Cut fabric strips ½" wider than the desired size of the diamond. For example, cut a 3½"-wide strip for a 3" finished diamond. Line up the tool on the selvedge end of the strip as shown, and trim the edge.

Step 2: Slide tool to right, completely filling the desired size diamond with fabric. Cut.

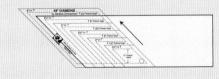

Step 3: Continue in this manner down the length of the strip.

Resources

The tools and supplies shown in this book are from the following manufacturers and can be found in your local quilt shop, fabric or craft store, on the Web, or by mail order.

American and Efird Inc.
(A&E Threads)
P.O. Box 507, Mt. Holly, NC 28120
(708) 822-6014
www.amefird.com

Robert Kaufman Fabrics, Inc.
129 W. 132nd St.
Los Angeles, CA 90061
(310) 538-3482
www.robertkaufman.com

EZ Quilting by Wrights
6050 Dana Way
Antioch, TN 37013-3116
(800) 660-0415
www.ezquilt.com

Fairfield Processing Corp.
P.O. Box 1157
Danbury, CT 06813-1157
(800) 980-8000
www.poly-fil.com

Hobbs Bonded Fibers
P.O. 2521
Waco, TX 76702-2521
(800) 433-3357
www.hobbsbondedfibers.com

Roxanne Products Company
742 Granite Ave.
Lathrop, CA 95330
(209) 983-8700
www.thatperfectstitch.com

Bernina of America
3702 Prairie Lake Court
Aurora, IL 60504
(630) 978-2500
email: jeanne@berninausa.com

Needlings, Inc.
P.O. Box 99
Fairfax, MN 55332
www.feedsacklady.com

CATALOGS

The tools and supplies shown in this book are also available from the following catalogs and websites.

Clotilde, LLC
P.O. Box 7500
Big Sandy, TX 75755-7500
(800) 772-2891
www.clotilde.com

Connecting Threads
P.O. Box 870760
Vancouver, WA 98687-7760
(800) 574-6454
www.connectingthreads.com

Keepsake Quilting
Route 25, P.O. Box 1618
Center Harbor, NH 03226-1618
(800) 438-5464
www.keepsakequilting.com

Nancy's Notions
333 Beichl Ave., P.O. Box 683
Beaver Dam, WI 53916-0683
(800) 833-0690
www.nancysnotions.com

Meet the Author

Acclaimed quilter, author and fabric designer Darlene Zimmerman teaches and lectures nationally and internationally. Darlene designs quilting tools for EZ Quilting by Wrights and multiple vintage-inspired fabric lines for Robert Kaufman Fabrics, Inc. She has written the books *Quick Quilted Miniatures, Granny Quilts, Granny Quilt Décor, Fat Quarter Small Quilts, The Quilter's Edge, and Quilting: The Complete Guide* with Krause Publications. She also designs patterns for Simplicity Pattern Company, Inc. and for her own company, Needlings, Inc. You will find Darlene's patterns featured frequently in many quilting magazines. Darlene resides in Minnesota with her husband. Visit Darlene at www. feedsacklady.com.

More Classic Quilting Know-How from Darlene

QUILTING THE COMPLETE GUIDE

by Darlene Zimmerman

Everything you need to know to quilt is in this book. More than 400 color photos and illustrations demonstrating the quilt making process.

Hardcover • 5⅝ x 7⅞ • 256 pages
400 color photos and illus.
Item# **Z0320** • **$29.99**

FAT QUARTER SMALL QUILTS

25 Projects You Can Make in a Day
by Darlene Zimmerman

Using "fat quarters", quilters will complete 25 projects including wall hangings, tablemats, doll quilts, gifts and more in a wide variety of themes. Most projects can be completed in less than a day!

Softcover • 8¼ x 10⅞ • 128 pages
250 color photos and illus.
Item# **FQSM** • **$21.99**

GRANNY QUILT DÉCOR

Vintage Quilts of the '30s inspire projects for today's home
by Darlene Zimmerman

Features quilting ideas for all skill levels, including bed-sized quilts, wall hangings, pillows, kitchen novelties and more. Discover more than 30 fantastic projects, and basic quilting instructions inside.

Softcover • 8¼ x 10⅞ • 128 pages
125 color photos, 150 illus.
Item# **GQDCR** • **$21.99**

THE QUILTER'S EDGE

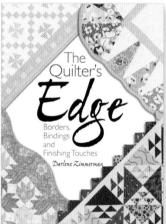

Borders, Bindings and Finishing Touches
by Darlene Zimmerman

Bring a fabulous finish to any quilt with more than 200 step-by-step instructional color photos covering techniques including scalloped edges, curved edges, notched edges and more.

Softcover • 8¼ x 10⅞ • 128 pages
200+ color photos and illus.
Item# **QLFT** • **$22.99**